The
Youth
of
Zion

The
Youth
of
Zion

Guidance from modern prophets
on dozens of timely topics
facing today's families

compiled by
Chad Daybell

CFI Books
Springville, Utah

ISBN: 1-55517-631-3
e.1

Published by CFI
An imprint of Cedar Fort Inc.
www.cedarfort.com

Distributed by:

Cover design by Adam Ford
Cover design © 2002 by Lyle Mortimer

"Jesus, Forgive Me" © 1989 Paul J. Daybell.

Printed in the United States of America
10 9 8 7 6 5 4 3 2 1

Printed on acid-free paper

Library of Congress Control Number: 2002093178

To Randy Killpack
and
Ray Huntington,
my first two Seminary teachers.

Their vibrant testimonies
changed my life.

Shall the youth of Zion falter
In defending truth and right?
While the enemy assaileth,
Shall we shrink or shun the fight?
No!
True to the faith
that our parents have cherished,
True to the truth
for which martyrs have perished,
To God's command,
Soul, heart and hand,
Faithful and true we will ever stand.

Written by Evan Stephens, 1854-1930
Verse 1 of "True to the Faith,"
Hymn #254 in the LDS Hymnbook

TABLE of CONTENTS

INTRODUCTION

The title of this book, *The Youth of Zion,* has two meanings. First, it speaks of the youth of the LDS Church, and their desire to live righteously. It also refers to the role that today's youth will play in the great events leading to the Second Coming of Jesus Christ, as the Church becomes a Zion society.

I have had the opportunity to work with the youth of the Church on several occasions as a Scoutmaster, and as a counselor in the Young Men's program. There were many times I wished the words of the prophets on certain topics were handy so I could share these ideas and statements with the young men.

This past year the need for such a book was brought to mind again—from the parents' point of view. Several of the men in our Elders Quorum have teenagers, and like any ward, some families are facing a few struggles.

One of my close friends, Gary, has had good success with his children, and he shared with our quorum some of his methods. If there is a dispute with his daughters over an issue that they just can't solve, they agree to turn to the words of the prophets.

This often takes a bit of effort on Gary's part, but once he finds a prophet's words on a subject, he and his children can read the statement together and decide what is the best option.

For example, one daughter wanted to wear a strapless gown to a school dance. Gary was able to find Spencer W. Kimball's words on modest dresses, and Gary's daughter accepted it. She chose a different, more modest dress to wear.

Gary's experience was an eye-opener to me about how we should be actively referring to the words of the prophets in our daily lives. The purpose of this book is to make those words more accessible on several of the key topics confronting the youth of the Church today.

In an effort to keep the book at a reasonable length, the topics were narrowed down into 34 chapters from an original list of 250 topics. While I feel some general topics, such as the priesthood, faith, and so forth, are vitally important to the gospel, they are also often the topics of lessons during Sunday meetings. These 34 topics were selected both for their importance and because they might not be frequently discussed on Sunday. They are truths that every member of the church—young and old—should understand.

The intent is to present the material in a way that a person can quietly read the book on their own, but possibly open a line of discussion later with family members or the bishop if there are further questions.

The vast majority of the book is adapted or taken directly from the words of the prophets, although I have occasionally included an interesting story, poem or personal experience to help the topic be more accessible.

Although there are quotations from all fifteen men who have served as President of The Church of Jesus Christ of Latter-day Saints through 2002, you will find three true champions of youth being quoted most prominently.

The first is President Gordon B. Hinckley, due to his current role as prophet, as well as his down-to-earth, straightforward approach to these topics.

The words of President Spencer W. Kimball are also used extensively. This prophet was small of stature, but he served as a powerful force for good. He was one of the greatest advocates for LDS youth, and sought to help them live clean, righteous lives.

And finally, the words of President Joseph F. Smith are often shared. President Smith holds an unusual place in LDS Church history. As the son of Hyrum Smith and the nephew of the Prophet Joseph Smith, he is a powerful link to the earliest days of the Church. He was born in 1838, endured the deaths of Hyrum and Joseph in 1844, and drove a wagon across the plains as a young boy. From that beginning he lived to see many marvelous changes in the world, such as the invention of the automobile and the airplane. His words ring of truth—emphasizing that the standards and teachings of the Church remain constant, despite the ever-changing beliefs and styles of the world.

In closing, I would like to include a statement from President Harold B. Lee that sums up the whole reason why prophets counsel us. He said:

"You may not like what comes from the authority of the Church. It may contradict your political views. It may contradict your social views. It may interfere with some of your social life. But if you listen to these things, as if from the mouth of the Lord himself, with patience and faith, the promise is that 'the gates of hell shall not prevail against you; yea, and the Lord God will disperse the powers of darkness from before you, and cause the heavens to shake for your good, and his name's glory.'" (D&C 21:6)[1]

What greater promise could we hope for?

Chad Daybell
July 15, 2002

Never forget that you were chosen
and brought to earth as a child of God
for something of importance
in His grand design.
He expects marvelous things of you.
He expects you to keep your life
clean from the sins of the world.

—President Gordon B. Hinckley
Youth Fireside Broadcast, Dec. 5, 1982

CHAPTER 1

ANGER

He that is slow to anger
is better than the mighty;
and he that ruleth his spirit
than he that taketh a city.
Proverbs 16:32

Momentary anger can have eternal consequences, even ruining lives and families. We hear of "road rage" and tragic incidents sparked by anger that would never happen if emotions had been kept under control. Even within our homes there are often examples of anger and violence.

President Gordon B. Hinckley said, "There is so much of argument in the homes of the people. It is so destructive. It is so corrosive. It leads only to bitterness, heartbreak, and tears. How well advised we would be, each of us, when there is tension, when there is friction, when there is affliction, to speak with consoling words in the spirit of meekness."[1]

Few of us have suffered as the Prophet Joseph Smith did on the night of March 25, 1832, in Hiram, Ohio. Would we have responded as calmly as Joseph did?

That spring night the Prophet and his wife Emma were anxiously caring for their eleven-month-old adopted twins, who were both very ill. Neither parent had received much rest. Joseph was completely worn out and finally fell asleep. Emma then heard a gentle tapping on the window. A few moments later an infuriated mob burst through the door and surrounded Joseph's bed. Ten men seized him and dragged him from the house.

As they were taking him through the door, Joseph made a desperate struggle to release himself, despite being greatly outnumbered. The mobbers used every form of profanity, and they declared they would kill him if he did not cease his struggles.

As the mob started around the house with him, one of the mobbers thrust his hands into the Prophet's face and shrieked at him. Then he seized Joseph's throat and choked him until he stopped breathing. When Joseph recovered from this attack, these wicked men continued to curse him and told him to ask his God for help.

They then dragged Joseph into a meadow. One of the mobbers asked the others if Joseph should be killed, but the leading mobocrats decided they would not kill him. Instead, they stripped him naked and whipped him, tearing his flesh.

Someone brought forth a bucket of tar and covered Joseph's body with the substance, then thrust the reeking tar paddle into his face. They attempted to force the paddle down his throat, but he kept his teeth tightly clenched. Then they tried to force a vial containing poison into his mouth, but it broke between his lips. One of the men then fell upon Joseph and began to tear at him like a wildcat, at the same time screaming, "That's the way the Holy Ghost falls on folks!"

The devilish mob finally left Joseph in the meadow. He tried to get up, but fell back from pain and exhaustion. He succeeded, however, in tearing the tar away from his face so that he could breathe, and shortly afterward he crawled toward a light and found that it came from his house. He eventually reached the door. When Emma saw his bruised, tar-covered body, she thought the tar was blood, causing her to scream—then faint.

Joseph found a blanket to cover himself, then he entered the house, where he and his friends spent the remainder of the night removing the tar and cleaning his injuries. The bottle that had been smashed into his mouth had chipped one of his front teeth, and for the rest of his life he would occasionally make a slight whistling sound when he spoke.

The morning after the attack was Sunday, and the Saints assembled at their meetings. With them came some of the mobbers, including Simonds Rider, an apostate who was the leader of the mob. Many others of the mob were also in attendance.

With his flesh all bruised and scarred, Joseph went to the meeting and stood before the congregation, calmly facing his assailants of the previous night. He preached a powerful sermon and later that same day baptized three people into the Church.[2]

What courage and emotional control the Prophet showed, especially to have his attackers right there at church with him! Throughout his life the Prophet Joseph controlled his anger, despite facing some of the strongest persecution a man has ever faced. Hopefully we can learn to do likewise.

And what about those men who tormented Joseph? What is the fate of men who became enraged enough to tear a man from his home in the middle of the night?

It brings to mind a statement by President Ezra Taft Benson, who said, "If a man does not control his temper, it is a sad admission that he is not in control of his thoughts. He then becomes a victim of his own passions and emotions, which lead him to actions that are totally unfit for civilized behavior, let alone behavior for a priesthood holder."[3]

Words to live by:

Joseph F. Smith: There would be no strife, no anger, nothing of the spirit of unforgiveness, unchastity and injustice, in the hearts of the children of men, if we loved the truth and obeyed it as it was taught by the Son of Man. With this spirit we could advance to the extreme position that we would pray for those who despitefully use us, who speak all manner of evil against us falsely, accuse us of wrongdoing, and lay plans and plots to bring us into disrepute. There would be no such desires in the hearts of the children of men, if they possessed the Spirit of the Lord Jesus Christ. There would be no contention, dishonor, nor dishonesty among neighbors nor in the communities of the people. None would take advantage of the unwary, the weak or unsuspecting; no one would seek to wrong another; but, on the contrary, we would feel like Jesus himself expressed it, "he that is greatest among you, let him be the servant of all."[4]

Wilford Woodruff: The moment a man or woman becomes angry, they show a great weakness.[5]

Brigham Young: If I bear an insult with meek patience, and do not return the injury, I have a decided advantage over my adversary. [6]

CHAPTER 2

CHARITY

But charity is the pure love of Christ,
and it endureth forever;
and whoso is found possessed of it
at the last day, it shall be well with him.
Moroni 7:47

Several religion instructors once took a summer college course about the life of the Savior. When it came time for the final exam, the students arrived at their classroom to find a note. It said the exam would be given in another building across the campus, and that the exam had to be completed within the two-hour time period that had already begun.

The religion instructors hurried across the campus. On the way they passed a little girl crying over a flat tire on her bike. Nearby, an old man hobbled painfully toward the library with a cane in one hand, spilling books every few feet from a large stack he was trying to carry with the other arm. As the instructors neared the other building, they saw a shabbily dressed, bearded man on a bench holding a sign that read, "I need money to eat. Please help me."

They all passed by, and rushed into the other classroom. The class members were met by their professor, who announced they had all flunked the final exam. He mentioned their missed opportunities—the little girl, the old man, the beggar—and then told them that the only true test of whether they understood the Savior's life and teachings was how they treated people in need.[1]

When our day of judgment comes, it will likely be the small and simple acts of kindness we gave that will show our true greatness, rather than the honors of the world. Such acts of charity were common among those men who would eventually lead the Church.

Joseph F. Smith's thoughtfulness for the elderly and his tender care for little children were among his most pronounced characteristics.

Elder Orson F. Whitney said of him, "I have known him to leave his place upon a railroad train to speak a word of comfort to a poor old lady whose feelings had been hurt by an ill-mannered conductor in some matter pertaining to her ticket. Once I saw him, when an excursion was just about to start, walk the full length of the crowded train, with no apparent object but to satisfy himself that everybody was comfortably seated, and not until every man, woman and child was provided for, did the President of the Church take his seat."[2]

Spencer W. Kimball also showed Christlike care for strangers about him. A young mother on an overnight flight with a two-year-old daughter was stranded by bad weather in a Chicago airport without food, clean clothing for the child, or money.

She was two months pregnant and threatened with miscarriage, so she was under doctor's instructions not to carry her daughter unless it was essential. Hour after hour she stood in one line after another, trying to get a flight to Michigan. The terminal was noisy and full of tired, grumpy passengers. The woman heard critical references to her crying child and about the fact she was sliding her daughter along the floor with her foot as the line moved forward. However, no one offered to help her out.

Then, the young mother later reported, "Someone came toward us and with a kindly smile said, 'Is there something I could do to help you?' With a grateful sigh I accepted his offer. He lifted my sobbing little daughter from the cold floor and lovingly held her to him while he patted her gently on the back. He asked if she could chew a piece of gum. When she was settled down, he carried her with him and said something kindly to the others in the line ahead of me, about how I needed their help.

"The other people seemed to agree, and he went up to the ticket counter at the front of the line and made arrangements with the clerk to put me on a flight leaving shortly. He walked with us to a bench, where we chatted a moment, until he was assured that I would be fine. He went on his way. About a week later I saw a picture of Apostle Spencer W. Kimball and recognized him as the stranger in the airport."[3]

A little kindness can go a long way! President Gordon B. Hinckley said, "Let us as Latter-day Saints cultivate a spirit of brotherhood in all of our associations. Let us be more charitable in our judgments, more sympathetic and understanding of those who err, more willing to forgive those who err, more willing to forgive those who trespass against us."[4]

Words to live by:

Joseph Smith: The nearer we get to our Heavenly Father, the more we are disposed to look with compassion on perishing souls; we feel that we want to take them upon our shoulders, and cast their sins behind our backs. If you would have God have mercy on you, have mercy on one another.[5]

CHAPTER 3

DANCING

If thou art merry, praise the Lord with singing,
with music, with dancing,
and with a prayer of praise and thanksgiving.
D&C 136: 28

The past few years have seen drastic changes in what the world views as acceptable dance styles. Elvis Presley's dance moves in the 1950s and Chubby Checker's "The Twist" in the 1960s caused parents to be outraged, but those dances now seem rather innocent. Standards have sadly slipped. The suggestive dance moves that many performers use today would have gotten them kicked out of the building not many years ago.

Despite the poor examples among today's entertainers, dancing itself is a wonderful thing—in the right way and setting. Church-sponsored dances provide a great place to meet new people and develop social skills.

Naturally, Satan would love for you to go beyond the boundaries of good taste, and many public dance clubs create an atmosphere for trouble. This is an area where you should let the Spirit be your guide, and get out of such situations if you feel uncomfortable.

President Spencer W. Kimball said, "The properly conducted dancing party can be a blessing. It provides opportunity to spend a pleasant evening with many people to the accompaniment of music. It can create and develop friendships which will be treasured in later years. Well-ordered dances provide favorable places, pleasing times, and auspicious circumstances in which to meet new people and to enlarge circles of friends. They can be an open door to happiness."

President Kimball does warn, "On the other hand, for a youth to dance all evening with one partner, which we might call 'monopolistic' dancing, is not only anti-social but it circumscribes one's legitimate pleasures and opportunities. Also it can encourage improper intimacies by its exclusiveness."[1]

President Gordon B. Hinckley has recently warned about a new form of dance party that has emerged in society—secret underground drug parties called "raves."

President Hinckley said, "Here with flashing lights and noisy music, if it can be called that, young men and women dance and sway. They sell and buy drugs. The drugs are called Ecstasy. They are a derivative of methamphetamine. The dancers suck on babies' pacifiers because the drug makes them grind their teeth. The hot music and the sultry dancing go on until 7:30 of a Sunday morning. What does it all lead to? Nowhere. It is a dead end."[2]

Use wisdom, and let dances be uplifting experiences for you, rather than ones you will later regret.

Words to live by:

Joseph F. Smith: No Latter-day Saint needs to be told that two or three dances a week for his children are out of all sense of reason. Home parties, concerts that develop the talents of youth, and public amusements that bring together both young and old, are preferable to the excessive practice of dancing.[3]

CHAPTER 4

DATING

*And that same sociality which exists
among us here will exist among us there,
only it will be coupled with eternal glory,
which glory we do not now enjoy.*
D&C 130:2

Dating can be a wonderful experience, meeting new people, having fun, and learning social skills such as courtesy and thoughtfulness. Of course, it also has the purpose of helping you find your future spouse!

There is truth to the statement, "You only marry someone you date." If celestial marriage is your goal, you will find it virtually impossible to get married in the temple if you date people who don't share that goal.

Elder Bruce R. McConkie often emphasized there are three key things to remember as you approach adulthood. These three keys will affect the rest of your life. They are:

1. **Marry the right person**
2. **In the right place** (the temple)
3. **By the right authority** (the Holy Priesthood)

Elder McConkie then adds, "The most important remaining thing that any Latter-day Saint can ever do is to live so that the terms and conditions of the covenant will be binding now and forever."[1]

If you promise yourself that you won't settle for less than a temple marriage, then items 2 and 3 are taken care of. You will be married in the House of the Lord by a person holding the authorized priesthood keys. What now remains is to find someone who shares your goals—and hopefully is someone you find attractive, fun and lovable.

So with those goals already set, the "dating game" should be much easier, and the odds are much better that you will win the most important game of all—gaining eternal life.

The prophets have given specific counsel in helping us stay on course. Their first advice is simple—wait.

Spencer W. Kimball said, "Any dating or pairing off in social contacts should be postponed until at least the age of 16 or older, and even then there should be much judgment used."[2]

President Hinckley adds, "The Church counsels against early dating. This rule is not designed to hurt you in any way. It is designed to help you, and it will do so if you will observe it.

"Steady dating at an early age leads so often to tragedy. Studies have shown that the longer a boy and girl date one another, the more likely they are to get into trouble.

"It is better, my friends, to date a variety of companions until you are ready to marry. Have a wonderful time, but stay away from familiarity. Keep your hands to yourself. It may not be easy, but it is possible."[3]

In my seventh grade Social Studies class I sat behind a pretty girl named Teri. She was so sweet and kind, and seemed to have the world ahead of her. It is safe to say that every boy in our grade had a crush on her.

School let out for the summer, and when we returned

that fall to begin eighth grade, I looked in the halls for Teri, because she would always say hello to me. After two days, I finally asked my friends, "Did Teri move away?"

One of them started laughing. "Haven't you heard?" he asked. "Teri quit school. She's pregnant!"

The news really shook me up. I had thought only really frightening girls got pregnant out of wedlock—not someone like Teri. But she had let her guard down over the summer, trusting a boy who didn't truly respect her.

President Kimball said it so well: "My beloved youth, he is not your friend who would rob you of your virtue. She does not love you if she tempts you or yields to you. Such is your enemy. To require the yielding to passion, and gratification, yet to profess love, is to lie; for we never exploit one whom we love."[4]

Concerning those precious high school years, President Gordon B. Hinckley said, "When you are young, do not get involved in steady dating. When you reach an age where you think of marriage, then is the time to become so involved. But you boys who are in high school don't need this, and neither do the girls."[5]

However, the time **will** come when it is proper to start dating. President Ezra Taft Benson gave a wonderful summary of what kind of partners LDS youth should be looking for. He was speaking to the young men of the Church, but it applies to young women as well.

He said, "Do not expect perfection in your choice of a mate. Do not be so particular that you overlook her most important qualities of having a strong testimony, living the principles of the gospel, loving home, wanting to be a mother in Zion, and supporting you in your priesthood responsibilities.

"Of course, she should be attractive to you, but do not

just date one girl after another for the sole pleasure of dating without seeking the Lord's confirmation in your choice of your eternal companion.

"And one good yardstick as to whether a person might be the right one for you is this: in her presence, do you think your noblest thoughts, do you aspire to your finest deeds, do you wish you were better than you are?"[6]

Words to live by:

Spencer W. Kimball: Dating—and especially steady dating—in the early teens is most hazardous. It distorts the whole picture of life. It deprives the youth of worthwhile and rich experiences; it limits friendships; it reduces the acquaintances which can be so valuable in selecting a partner for time and eternity.[7]

Joseph F. Smith: Some people feel that it does not make very much difference whether a girl marries a man in the Church, full of faith in the Gospel, or an unbeliever. Some of our young people have married outside of the Church; but very few of those who have done it have failed to come to grief. . . . There is nothing I can think of, in a religious way, that would grieve me more intensely than to see one of my boys marry an unbelieving girl, or one of my girls marry an unbelieving man.[8]

Brigham Young: How is it with you, sisters? Do you distinguish between a man of God and a man of the world? It is one of the strangest things that happens in my existence, to think that any man or woman can love a being that will not receive the truth of heaven.[9]

CHAPTER 5

DISCOURAGEMENT

Peace I leave with you,
my peace I give unto you:
not as the world giveth, give I unto you.
Let not your heart be troubled,
neither let it be afraid.
John 14:27

When I was a teenager, I became friends with Milt Harrison, an elderly man who lived around the corner. He always had a positive attitude, even though he couldn't move his legs and was confined to a wheelchair. I had noticed the ring finger on his left hand was missing, and one day I got up enough courage to ask him what had happened.

He smiled and said, "I've been waiting for you to ask." He held up his hand and showed me the space where a finger should have been.

"One day when I was ten years old I was walking along Hobble Creek," he said. "I came to a barbed wire fence. I either had to climb the fence or go back the way I had come, so I climbed the fence. As I grabbed the top strand of wire, my feet slipped out from under me. I was wearing a cheap little ring that I thought was fancy, and when I slipped the ring got caught on one of the fence barbs. Before I knew it, off went my finger!"

His voice became much more serious as he then described how he had hurried home holding his injured hand, and how the town doctor had to cut off the remaining part of his finger. The injury soon became infected, and Milt developed polio, a disease that often led to paralysis or even death. In Milt's case, his legs were severely weakened.

Milt was bedridden for many months, but finally he developed enough strength to go back to school. That was almost as terrible, as the other children mocked him for his missing finger and the crutches he used.

The story surprised me, because I knew Milt had accomplished many things in his life—such as graduating from BYU, having a successful accounting career, serving on the city council, marrying a lovely wife and raising two daughters.

"Wow," I said. "I probably would have given up. What gave you the courage to accomplish what you did?"

"Oh I got discouraged at times," Milt said, "but no matter what other people said about me, I knew my Savior loved me. I knew he didn't care whether I had ten fingers or nine, or if my legs worked. When I attended BYU, I had to make my way up the paths to the different buildings using a wooden walker, since I couldn't carry my books using crutches.

"The first day it took me an hour to get to my first class, but by the end of the semester I could get there in 25 minutes! And that's the way I've lived my life. The only race is with yourself."

It would have been a tragedy if Milt had just given up on life as a young man, figuring his physical challenges were just too much. Thankfully he found someone to lean on—the Savior. Milt has passed away, but he left a legacy of determination. The poem on the following page makes me think of Milt.

Don't Be Afraid to Fail

You've failed many times,
Although you may not remember.
You fell down the first time you tried to walk.
You almost drowned the first time
You tried to swim, didn't you?
Did you hit the ball the first time you swung a bat?
Heavy hitters, the ones who hit the most home runs,
Also strike out a lot.
R.H. Macy failed seven times
Before his store in New York caught on.
English novelist John Creasy got 753 rejection slips
Before he published 564 books.
Babe Ruth struck out 1,330 times,
But he also hit 714 home runs.
Don't worry about failure.
Worry about the chances you miss
When you don't even try.

—Author unknown

How we respond to challenges—whether we control them, or let them control us—will determine the course of our lives. President Gordon B. Hinckley has said, "Please don't nag yourself with thoughts of failure. Do not set goals far beyond your capacity to achieve. Simply do what you can do, in the best way you know, and the Lord will accept your effort."[1]

President Ezra Taft Benson said, "The key to overcoming aloneness and a feeling of uselessness is to step outside yourself by helping others who are truly needy. We promise those who will render this kind of service that, in some measure, you will be healed of the loss of loved ones or the dread of being alone. The way to feel better about your own situation is to improve someone else's circumstances."[2]

Few church leaders ever faced such an uphill battle to success as Heber J. Grant. His father died when he was very young, and being an only child, his mother reared him very carefully—in Heber's mind, maybe too carefully.

Heber described himself as a boy as "long and lanky, but not substantial." He learned to sweep the floor and wash dishes, but he did little stone throwing and rarely participated in those sports which are interesting and attractive to boys, and which develop their strength.

Concerning his first baseball season, he said, "When I joined a baseball club, the boys of my own age and a little older played in the first nine; those younger than I played in the second, and those still younger in the third, and I played with them.

"One of the reasons for this was that I could not throw the ball from one base to the other. Another reason was that I lacked physical strength to run or bat well. When I picked up a ball, the boys would generally shout, "Throw it here, sissy!'"

The other boys teased Heber so badly that he solemnly vowed that he would someday play on a baseball team that would win the championship of the Territory of Utah.

Heber's mother was renting some rooms at the time to some men, and Heber shined their boots until he saved a dollar, which he invested in a baseball.

Heber said, "I spent hours and hours throwing the ball at Bishop Edwin D. Woolley's barn, which caused him to refer to me as the 'laziest boy in the Thirteenth Ward.' Often my arm would ache so that I could scarcely go to sleep at night. But I kept on practicing and finally succeeded in getting into the second nine of our club. Subsequently I joined a better club, and eventually played in the nine that won the championship of the territory and beat the nine that had won the championship for California, Colorado, and Wyoming. Having thus made good my promise to myself, I retired from the baseball arena."[3]

Heber used that same determination to become better at many things, most notably his handwriting. He said his handwriting once looked like "chicken scratch," but later he was well-known for his penmanship.

He was never a talented singer, but he tried throughout his life to become tolerable at it. Finally when he was President of the Church, he had improved enough to carry a tune. Now that is perseverance!

Words to live by:

Lorenzo Snow: When you find yourselves a little gloomy, look around you and find somebody that is in a worse plight than yourself. Go to him and find out what the trouble is, then try to remove it with the wisdom which the Lord bestows upon you; and the first thing you know, your gloom is gone, you feel light, the Spirit of the Lord is upon you, and everything seems illuminated.[4]

Brigham Young: The most inferior person now upon the earth is worth worlds.[5]

CHAPTER 6
EDUCATION and EMPLOYMENT

Whatever principle of intelligence we attain
unto in this life, it will rise with us in the resurrection.
And if a person gains more knowledge
and intelligence in this life through his diligence
and obedience than another, he will have
so much the advantage in the world to come.
D&C 130: 18-19

We have all been sent to earth with different talents. I am able to write, but anything beyond basic math strains my brain. I am also completely unskilled when it comes to drawing a picture. My six-year-old son draws better pictures than I do.

Maybe you are the same way—strong in some areas, while not as strong in others. So as you pursue your life's profession, seek out a career you like and that will use one of your talents.

The same principle applies when it comes to gaining an education. People hear the word "education" and automatically think of a college degree. That isn't necessarily the case.

President Howard W. Hunter said, "The employment we chose should be honorable and challenging. Ideally, we need to seek that work to which we are suited by interest, by aptitude, and by training. A man's work should do more than provide adequate income; it should provide him with a sense of self-worth and be pleasurable—

something he looks forward to each day."[1]

My father is an electrician, and as a child I felt duty-bound to become one, too. It made me nervous, though, because as I mentioned, I don't have a mechanical mind. Words like *watt*, *volt*, and *circuit breaker* sounded complicated. So it came as a surprise and relief when one day Dad told me I didn't have to be an electrician.

Heavenly Father is not so worried about **what** you do for a living, as much as **how** you do your job, and whether it affects how you live the gospel.

I like this story from the life of Joseph Fielding Smith. He showed wisdom at a young age that others often take a lifetime to acquire.

When Joseph was newly married, he had a job that hardly paid enough to support himself and his wife, so he was eager to try something else. About this time he was offered a job as a traveling representative. His area would cover much of the western United States. The starting salary was exceptionally good. It was a tempting offer, even though it would require him to associate with people whose standards were not always in keeping with his.

Joseph asked the company president why the position had become available. The president said the previous employee had been discharged for succumbing to the temptations connected with the work environment. Joseph was being offered the position because the president felt Joseph would be above temptation and could be trusted.

It didn't take Joseph long to make his decision—he chose not to take the job, which came as a great surprise to the employer. Joseph chose the path that would most likely keep him in tune with Heavenly Father, rather than purposely putting himself in tempting situations—despite the company president's belief that Joseph was above temptation. Joseph knew better than to take that chance.

Joseph soon found a decent job—not one that would make him rich, as the other one would have—but that allowed him to build his new marriage and avoid the temptations of the world.[2]

With those guidelines in mind, the Lord does expect us to do the best we can in life. President Gordon B. Hinckley has said, "Get all the education that you can. The Lord has laid upon you a mandate that you should learn, that you should study, that you should acquire knowledge of things beneath the earth and above the earth and in the earth, of history and kingdoms and countries and cultures. . . . That is a revelation to you, that you should acquire knowledge, and the marvelous thing is that as you acquire knowledge, your capacity will increase. You will be more widely recognized by people of the society in which you live. You simply reflect honor to this Church and build a wonderful name in promoting it."[3]

We must reach our potential and use our talents, moving to a different job as our skills improve and opportunities come our way. I certainly wouldn't be reaching my potential if I was still clinging to one of my first jobs—emptying garbage cans each night at a local park.

Every time I smell Kentucky Fried Chicken, it still reminds me of those seemingly endless rows of garbage cans filled to the top with chicken bones each summer night. But it also reminds me how far I've progressed in my professional life.

It is important to be patient—no one starts at the top of the employment chain. But working hard at a so-called "bad" job can pave the way to better things.

Through prayer, and by listening to the Spirit, the

Lord will guide you to the educational and employment opportunities that best suit you.

The following words by President Ezra Taft Benson are the key to attaining our educational goals. He said, "We must put God in the forefront of everything else in our lives. . . . When we put God first, all other things fall into their proper place or drop out of our lives."[4]

Words to live by:

Spencer W. Kimball: We encourage our people to study and prepare to render service with their minds and with their hands. Some are inclined toward formal university training, and some are inclined toward practical vocational training. We feel that our people should receive that kind of training which is most consistent with their interest and talents. Whether it be in the professions, the arts, or the vocations; whether it be university or vocational training, we applaud and encourage it.[5]

Joseph F. Smith: The mere stuffing of the mind with a knowledge of facts is not education. The mind must not only possess a knowledge of the truth, but the soul must revere it, cherish it, love it as a priceless gem; and this human life must be guided and shaped by it in order to fulfill its destiny.[6]

CHAPTER 7

ENTERTAINMENT CHOICES

And as all have not faith, seek ye diligently
and teach one another words of wisdom;
yea, seek ye out of the best books words of wisdom;
seek learning, even by study and also by faith. ...
Therefore, cease from all your light speeches,
from all laughter, from all your lustful desires,
from all your pride and light-mindedness,
and from all your wicked doings.
D&C 88:118, 121

The above scripture in many ways seems aimed at the Saints today as much as the Saints in the 1830s. The members of the church in Joseph Smith's time would likely be overwhelmed by the entertainment choices we have today.

In pioneer times, the youth entertained themselves with outdoor games such as stick pulling and races, while indoors they would read books and tell stories. Unfortunately, today we seem to require greater stimuli to avoid being bored. But must it be that way?

More entertainment isn't necessarily better, especially if it is degrading and doesn't allow us to feel the Holy Ghost. The following words by President Gordon B. Hinckley hit the mark, especially when it comes to our daily entertainment choices. He said, "The course of our lives is not determined by great, awesome decisions. Our direction is set by the little day-to-day choices which chart the track on which we run."[1]

President Ezra Taft Benson declared, "The Book of Mormon declares that 'every thing which inviteth and enticeth to do good, and to love God, and to serve him, is inspired of God.' (Moroni 7:13) . . . Let us use that standard to judge what we read, the music we hear, the entertainment we watch, the thoughts we think. Let us be more Christlike."[2]

As our entertainment opportunities seem to multiply with each passing year, the prophets have given us guidance, especially with the spread of home video and the Internet. Their suggestions may prompt ideas about how to make your home a place where entertainment is uplifting and in harmony with the Spirit.

Books

When President Hinckley was a boy he lived in a large old house. One room was called the library. It had a solid table and a good lamp, three or four comfortable chairs with good light, and books in cases that lined the walls. There were many volumes—the acquisitions of his parents over a period of many years.

The children were never forced to read them, but the books were placed where they were handy and where the children could get at them whenever they wished. President Hinckley said, "There was quiet in that room. It was understood that it was a place to study. . . . I would not have you believe that we were great scholars. But we were exposed to great literature, great ideas from great thinkers, and the language of men and women who thought deeply and wrote beautifully."[3]

President Hinckley has also said parents cultivate within their children a taste for the best literature. He said, "While they are very young, read to them the great stories which have become immortal because of the virtues they teach. Expose them to good books. Let there be a corner somewhere in your house, be it ever so small, where they will see at least a few books of the kind upon which great minds have been nourished."[4]

Joseph F. Smith spoke of the value of books not only for children, but adults as well. He said, "Read good books. Learn to sing and recite, and to converse upon subjects that will be of interest to your associates, and at your social gatherings, instead of wasting the time in senseless practices that lead only to mischief and sometimes to serious evil and wrongdoing; instead of this, seek out of the best books knowledge and understanding.

"Read history. Read philosophy, if you wish. Read anything that is good, that will elevate the mind and will add to your stock of knowledge, that those who associate with you may feel an interest in your pursuit of knowledge and of wisdom."[5]

Internet

Modern technology has brought us ways to communicate that would have seemed like science fiction just a few years ago. These advances have brought forth much good, including the Church's websites **www.lds.org** and **www.familysearch.org**, where people receive news about the Church and can research their ancestors for temple work. Nearly every corner of the civilized world has Internet access, and this has helped the Church become known in areas it has never before.

Of course, with many such modern conveniences, people have found ways to use this marvelous invention for evil. Thankfully, our prophets have warned us of the dangers.

In the October 2000 General Conference, President Hinckley warned those who had become involved in pornography on the Internet. He said, "I fear this may be going on in some of your homes. It is vicious. It is lewd and filthy. It is enticing and habit-forming. It will take a young man or woman down to destruction as surely as anything in this world. It is foul sleaze that makes its exploiters wealthy, its victims impoverished."

President Hinckley then warned parents to beware of the dangers that lurk there. He said, "I regret to say that many fathers themselves like to hear the siren song of those who peddle filth. Some of them also work the Internet for that which is lewd and lascivious."

He continued, "If there be any man within the sound of my voice who is involved in this or who is moving in this direction, I plead with you to get it out of your life. Get away from it. Stay away from it. Otherwise it will become an obsession. It will destroy your home life. It will destroy your marriage. It will take the good and beautiful out of your family relationships and replace these with ugliness and suspicion."

Then President Hinckley specifically addressed the youth of the Church. He said, "To you young men, and to the young women who are your associates, I plead with you not to befoul your minds with this ugly and vicious stuff. It is designed to titillate you, to absorb you into its net. It will take the beautiful out of your life. It will lead you into the dark and ugly. . . . Our youth find this tempting stuff all about them. They need the help of their parents in resisting it. They need a tremendous amount of self-control. They need the strength of good friends. They need prayer to fortify them against this flood tide of filth."[6]

Movies/Videos

A similar concern is raised concerning movies. Church leaders have long emphasized that Church members should not watch R-rated movies and videos. But as society's standards steadily slip, the emphasis has been made that we should also avoid movies that are vulgar, violent or promote immorality. Many PG-13-rated movies fall into this category. With the availability of online and newspaper reviews for nearly any movie or video, there isn't much excuse to watch one and then be "surprised" at improper content.

President Hinckley cautions, "These magazines, these videotapes, these late-night programs—you don't need them. They will just hurt you; they won't help you. They will destroy you if you persist in looking at them."[7]

Television

Television is another wonderful invention that is filled with good programs. President Hinckley has said, "I regard television as perhaps the greatest tool yet created to teach and educate people in large numbers."

He then added, "But I decry the filth, the rot, the violence, and the profanity that spew from television screens into our homes. It is a sad commentary on our societies. The fact that the television set is on six or seven hours every day in many homes says something of tremendous importance. I feel sorry for those who are addicted to the tube. I believe it is an addiction. It becomes a habit as pernicious as many other bad habits."[8]

Parents and children can decide together what is appropriate in their home. President Ezra Taft Benson suggests that families take the initiative against entertainment they find offensive.

He said, "Successful parents have found that it is not easy to rear children in an environment polluted with evil. Therefore, they may take deliberate steps to provide the best of wholesome influences. Moral principles are taught. Good books are made available and read. Television watching is controlled. Good and uplifting music is provided. But most importantly, the scriptures are read and discussed."[9]

President Spencer W. Kimball was also aware of the negative effects some television and radio programs could have on the youth of the Church. He said, "Be concerned about the types of programs your family is watching on television or hearing on radio. There is so much today that is unsavory and degrading, so much that gives the impression that the old sins of Sodom and Gomorrah are the 'in thing' to do today."[10]

Let the Holy Ghost be your guide and help you decide what you will allow into your mind—rather than sitting back and letting Satan's followers make that decision for you.

Words to live by:

Gordon B. Hinckley: I feel sorry for parents who do not read to their young children. I feel sorry for children who do not learn the wonders to be found in good books, or how stimulating an experience it is to get into the mind of a great thinker as that person expresses himself or herself, with language cultivated and polished, concerning great and important issues.[11]

Spencer W. Kimball: We need to constantly guard against immorality, pornography, and sexual permissiveness that would destroy the purity of the family members, young and old. What must we do? We must be constantly alert to their evil presence in our homes and destroy them as we would the germs and filth of disease. We must hunt them from the closets of our minds, freeing ourselves of such worldliness quenching the embers of wickedness before they become destructive flames.

How do we do this? There is only one sure way and that is through the gospel of the Lord Jesus Christ and being obedient to its profound and inspired teachings. Surely we must be made to realize that the purchase price of a family hearth free of such evil influences is the keeping of the commandments of God.[12]

Joseph F. Smith: Young people in their recreation should strive to form a love for that which will not be injurious. It is not true that the only recreation that can be enjoyed is that which is detrimental to the body and spirit.

We should train ourselves to find pleasure in that which invigorates, not stupefies and destroys the body; that which leads upward and not down; that which brightens, not dulls and stunts the intellect; that which elevates and exalts the spirit, not that clogs and depresses it. So shall we please the Lord, enhance our own enjoyment, and save ourselves and our children from impending sins.[13]

CHAPTER 8

FAMILY

*I have commanded you to bring up
your children in light and truth.*
D&C 93:40

For good or bad, you will be linked to your family throughout your life. Friends that seem inseparable now might suddenly no longer be part of your life with a simple change in circumstances. And to your surprise, your annoying little sister might turn out to be your best friend fifteen years from now!

The family unit is Heavenly Father's way of raising righteous people. It is the plan that is followed in heaven, and is the best way to live the gospel on earth.

President Ezra Taft Benson said, "The greatest joys in life are centered in the family, honorable marriage, and rearing a righteous posterity."[1]

The eternal nature of the family is a real thing. You almost certainly knew your family in the premortal world, and looked forward to your future on earth together. President Spencer W. Kimball said, "It is important for us to cultivate in our own family a sense that we belong together eternally, that whatever changes outside our home, there are fundamental aspects of our relationship which will never change."[2]

There was a time President George Albert Smith became very ill, and he had an experience that emphasized to him the importance of family—and upholding the family name.

He became so weak that he could barely move. It was an exhausting effort for him to even turn over in bed.

Under these conditions, he lost consciousness and passed to the other side. He said, "I found myself standing with my back to a large and beautiful lake, facing a great forest of trees. There was no one in sight, and there was no boat upon the lake or any other visible means to indicate how I might have arrived there. I realized, or seemed to realize, that I had finished my work in mortality and had gone home. I began to look around, to see if I could not find someone. There was no evidence of anyone living there, just those great, beautiful trees in front of me and the wonderful lake behind me.

"I began to explore, and soon I found a trail through the woods which seemed to have been used very little, and which was almost obscured by grass. I followed this trail, and after I had walked for some time and had traveled a considerable distance through the forest, I saw a man coming toward me. I became aware that he was a very large man, and I hurried my steps to reach him, because I recognized him as my grandfather. In mortality he weighed over three hundred pounds, so you may know he was a large man. I remember how happy I was to see him coming. I had been given his name and had always been proud of it.

"When Grandfather came within a few feet of me, he stopped. His stopping was an invitation for me to stop. Then—and this I would like the boys and girls and young people never to forget—he looked at me very earnestly and said, 'I would like to know what you have done with my name.'

"Everything I had ever done passed before me as though it were a flying picture on a screen—*everything* I had done. Quickly this vivid retrospect came down to the very time I was standing there. My whole life had passed before me. I smiled and looked at my grandfather and said, 'I have never done anything with your name of which you need be ashamed.'

"He stepped forward and took me in his arms, and as he did so, I became conscious again of my earthly surroundings. My pillow was as wet as though water had been poured on it—wet with tears of gratitude that I could answer unashamed.

"I have thought of this many times, and I want to tell you that I have been trying, more than ever since that time, to take care of that name. So I want to say to the boys and girls, to the young men and women, to the youth of the Church and of all the world: Honor your fathers and your mothers. Honor the names that you bear, because someday you will have the privilege and the obligation of reporting to them (and to your Father in Heaven) what you have done with their name."[3]

Parents have a duty to teach their children the gospel. Joseph Fielding Smith said, "Brethren and sisters, teach your children from their infancy to believe in Jesus Christ as our Redeemer, in Joseph Smith as prophet of God, and in his successors in this kingdom, and let them grow up with a knowledge of this truth in their hearts built upon faith and obedience to the commandments the Lord has given us."[4]

And President Spencer W. Kimball adds, "The time will come when only those who believe deeply and actively in the family will be able to preserve their families in the midst of the gathering evil."[5]

Family histories

One of the most important things a person can do is leave a life history for their family. It doesn't have to be fancy, but should include at least a basic outline of key dates and memories, including those of your parents if they have passed away. These seemingly unimportant details will mean a great deal to future generations.

President Spencer W. Kimball said, "I urge all of the people of this church to give serious attention to their family histories, to encourage their parents and grandparents to write their journals, and let no family go into eternity without having left their memoirs for their children, their grandchildren and their posterity."

He added, "This is a duty and a responsibility, and I urge every person to start the children out writing a personal history and journal."[6]

Family Home Evening

Family Home Evening was first introduced in 1915 by President Joseph F. Smith. As the years have rolled by, the wisdom and inspiration to have a "family night" has become clear. The Church does not schedule meetings or activities on Monday night. This is so families can spend that evening together discussing gospel topics and enjoying each other's company.

President Spencer W. Kimball said, "Regarding our home evenings, an evening home with the family or an evening out to some place of interest with your family only partly solves the need of the home evening. The teaching of the children the way of life is vitally important. Merely going to a show or a party together, or fishing, only half satisfies the real need, but to stay home and teach the children the gospel, the scriptures, and love for each other and love for their parents is most important."[7]

President Harold B. Lee commented, "This 'Home Evening' should be devoted to prayer, singing hymns, songs, instrumental music, scripture reading, family topics and specific instructions on the principles of the Gospel, and on the ethical problems of life, as well as on the duties and obligations of children to parents, the home, the Church, society, and the nation."[8]

Words to live by:

Harold B. Lee: The most important part of the Lord's work that you will do, is the work that you do within the walls of your own home.[9]

David O. McKay: No other success can compensate for failure in the home. The poorest shack in which love prevails over a united family is of greater value to God and future humanity than any other riches. In such a home God can work miracles and will work miracles. [10]

Joseph F. Smith: Far too many risk their children's spiritual guidance to chance, or to others rather than to themselves, and think that organizations suffice for religious training. Our temporal bodies would soon become emaciated if we fed them only once a week, or twice, as some of us are in the habit of feeding our spiritual and religious bodies.

Our material concerns would be less thriving if we looked after them only two hours a week, as some people seem to do with their spiritual affairs, especially if we in addition contented ourselves, as some do in religious matters, to let others look after them. No; on the other hand, this should be done every day, and in the home, by precept, teaching and example.

Brethren, there is too little religious devotion, love and fear of God, in the home; too much worldliness, selfishness, indifference and lack of reverence in the family, or these never would exist so abundantly on the outside. Then, the home is what needs reforming. Try today, and tomorrow, to make a change in your home by praying twice a day with your family; call on your children and your wife to pray with you. Ask a blessing upon every meal you eat.

Spend ten minutes in reading a chapter from the words of the Lord in the Bible, the Book of Mormon, the Doctrine and Covenants, before you retire, or before you go to your daily toil. Feed your spiritual selves at home, as well as in public places. Let love, and peace, and the Spirit of the Lord, kindness, charity, sacrifice for others, abound in your families.

Banish harsh words, envyings, hatreds, evil speaking, obscene language and innuendo, blasphemy, and let the Spirit of God take possession of your hearts. Teach to your children these things, in spirit and power, sustained and strengthened by personal practice. Let them see that you are earnest, and practice what you preach. . .

Not one child in a hundred would go astray, if the home environment, example and training, were in harmony with the truth in the gospel of Christ, as revealed and taught to the Latter-day Saints. Fathers and mothers, you are largely to blame for the infidelity and indifference of your children. You can remedy the evil by earnest worship, example, training and discipline, in the home.[11]

CHAPTER 9

FASTING

Nevertheless they did fast and pray oft,
and did wax stronger and stronger in their humility,
and firmer and firmer in the faith of Christ,
unto the filling their souls with joy and consolation,
yea, even to the purifying
and the sanctification of their hearts . . .
Helaman 3:35

The above scripture is talking about a time similar to ours. The prophet Helaman and his people were trying to do what is right, even as their society began to fall under the influence of evil men. One of the ways these men stayed in tune with Heavenly Father during challenging times was through fasting.

Fasting is a way to purify and humble ourselves, as well as bless others. The first Sunday of each month is designated by the Church as Fast Sunday. Members are expected to not eat for a period of two meals, then donate the value of those meals to the Church. That money is then used to help those who are struggling financially.

President Gordon B. Hinckley said, "It is not a burden to refrain from two meals a month and give the value thereof to assist in caring for the poor. It is, rather, a blessing. Not only will physical benefits flow from the observance of this principle, but spiritual values also. Our program of the fast day and the fast offering is so simple and so beautiful that I cannot understand why people everywhere do not take it up."[1]

Fasting isn't necessarily easy the first time, but as we continue to fast each month, it becomes a chance to renew ourselves spiritually.

President Howard W. Hunter said, "To discipline ourselves through fasting brings us in tune with God, and fast day provides an occasion to set aside the temporal so that we might enjoy the higher qualities of the spiritual. As we fast on that day we learn and better understand the needs of those who are less fortunate."[2]

Words to live by:

Spencer W. Kimball: We wish to remind all the Saints of the blessings that come from observing the regular fast and contributing as generous a fast offering as we can, and as we are in a position to give. Wherever we can, we could give many times the value of the meals from which we abstained.

This principle of promise, when lived in the spirit thereof, greatly blesses both giver and receiver. Upon practicing the law of the fast, one finds a personal well-spring of power to overcome self-indulgence and selfishness.[3]

Joseph F. Smith: Do not go beyond what is wise and prudent in fasting and prayer. The Lord can hear a simple prayer offered in faith, in half a dozen words, and he will recognize fasting that may not continue more than twenty-four hours just as readily as he will answer a prayer of a thousand words and fasting for a month.[4]

CHAPTER 10

FORGIVENESS

Verily, verily, I say unto you, my servants,
that inasmuch as you have forgiven
one another your trespasses,
even so I, the Lord, forgive you.
D&C 82:1

The supreme example of forgiveness is Jesus Christ's compassion for the Roman soldiers who were driving the nails into his hands and feet during the crucifixion. Jesus asked Heavenly Father to forgive them, because they didn't understand that they were killing the Son of God.

Read again the scripture at the top of this page. It indicates we will be forgiven by the Lord according to the forgiveness we give to others. Forgiveness can sometimes be a tough task, but it also helps us develop qualities that will allow us to become like Heavenly Father.

President Gordon B. Hinckley has said, "We are not without critics, some of whom are mean and vicious. We have always had them, and I suppose we will have them all through the future. But we shall go forward, returning good for evil, being helpful and kind and generous. I remind you of the teachings of our Lord concerning these matters. You are all acquainted with them. Let us be good people. Let us be friendly people. Let us be neighborly people. Let us be what members of The Church of Jesus Christ of Latter-day Saints ought to be."[1]

Heber J. Grant shared the challenge he faced to forgive a man who had been cut off from the Church for adultery, and who later asked to be rebaptized. President John Taylor had written a letter to the brethren who would be part of the church court, in which he wrote, "I want every man to vote his own convictions, and not to vote to make it unanimous unless it is unanimous."

When the matter was presented and voted upon by the church court, the vote stood evenly divided on his rebaptism. At a later time, the man came up again, and now a majority were in favor of his being baptized.

Finally, all of the men who were on the court voted to let him be rebaptized except one—a young Heber J. Grant. President John Taylor sent for him and said, "How will you feel when you meet the Lord, if this man is permitted to come up and say he repented although his sins were as scarlet, and you refused to let him be baptized?"

Heber told the prophet, "I will look the Lord squarely in the eye, and I will tell Him that any man that can destroy the virtue of a girl and then lie and claim that she was maligning him and blackmailing him, will never get back into this Church with my vote."

Heber then walked to his home, only one block away. He picked up his scriptures, and instead of it opening at the bookmark, it opened at the passage:

Wherefore, I say unto you, that ye ought to forgive one another; for he that forgiveth not his brother his trespasses standeth condemned before the Lord; for there remaineth in him the greater sin. I the Lord, will forgive whom I will forgive, but of you it is required to forgive all men. (D&C 64:9-10)

Heber shut the book, rushed back to President Taylor's office and said, "I give my consent."

President Taylor laughed in surprise. "My gracious, Heber, this is remarkable; what has happened?"

Heber told him what he had read, and President Taylor said, "Heber, when you left here a few minutes ago did you not think, 'What if he had defiled my wife or daughter?' And when you thought that didn't you feel as if you would like to just knock the life out of that man?"

Heber said, "I certainly did."

"How do you feel now?"

"Well, really and truly, I hope the poor old sinner can be forgiven."

"You feel a whole lot better, don't you?"

Heber said, "I certainly do."

President Taylor said, "You have learned a good lesson, that this Gospel is one of forgiveness of sin, of awful sin, if there is true repentance, and it brings peace into your heart when you forgive the sinner. It brings peace when you love the man that you hated, provided the man turns to doing right. You have learned a lesson in your youth. Never forget it."[2]

Of course, there are times we ourselves need to repent and ask forgiveness of the Lord. This should be a daily experience, as we grow and improve. It is through our Savior Jesus Christ that repentance is even possible.

My brother Paul is a well-liked, happy person who has blessed the lives of many people. His constant energy and enthusiasm is contagious.

Paul also has a quiet, spiritual side, and when he was in the Missionary Training Center, his relationship with the Savior truly deepened. One night, Paul felt inspired to write the following poem:

Jesus, Forgive Me

Nearly dead, down the road, He dragged the cross.
The people who laughed didn't realize the loss;
These people stood around and mocked . . .
If they only knew how much they once loved Him
To see him they would have flocked.
For this was Jesus Christ, the Savior of us all;
The one who would save us from that great fall.
As they drove the nails through His trembling hands,
The pain He felt began to fulfill His Father's plan.
There the Master of the world hung, alone;
Because for all men's sins He would atone.
As the people mocked, even as the spear went through,
All He could say was,
"Father, forgive them, for they know not what they do."
Through sin everyone has hurt Jesus, this is true;
I have to ask myself, am I mocking too?
For this, the pain in my heart is not too hard to see,
I only pray I'm heard when I say, "Jesus, forgive me!"

—*Paul J. Daybell*

Words to live by:

David O. McKay: Has somebody offended you in the Church? You may hold resentment if you wish, say nothing to him, and let resentment canker your soul. If you do, you will be the one who will be injured, not the one who you think has injured you. You will feel better and be far happier to follow the divine injunction: If you have aught against your brother, go to him. [3]

Joseph F. Smith: We ought to say in our hearts, let God judge between me and thee, but as for me I will forgive.[4]

CHAPTER 11

FRIENDS

Thy friends do stand by thee,
and they shall hail thee again
with warm hearts and friendly hands.
D&C 121:9

During the winter of 1839, Joseph Smith was unjustly imprisoned in Missouri's Liberty Jail. The jail was actually more like a dungeon, and for several months Joseph and a few companions suffered there. At his greatest moment of despair, Joseph cried out to the Lord, and the Lord answered his prayer with what has become D&C sections 121 and 122. And in the above scripture, the Lord let Joseph know that his friends were still there for him.

A true friend is invaluable, especially because few factors determine your future as do your teenage friends. They can lift you to great heights, or drag you into the misery of sin.

President Spencer W. Kimball had some friends who weren't doing the right things. They were doing a little stealing, and violating the Word of Wisdom.

Fourteen-year-old Spencer saw what was going on in their lives, went to his room, got on his knees, and told the Lord that he would not do those things. And having once made that decision, he never had to make it again.[1]

I faced a similar situation as a teenager. I had a friend named Dave who came from a good family, and who had a great future ahead of him. There was a group of us who would play basketball or golf after school, and Dave was one of the better players. But Dave became curious about drugs. He thought they might help him do better in school and at sports. He found ways to get some marijuana, and he started smoking it at night.

The rest of us realized Dave was heading down the wrong path, and we encouraged him to stop doing drugs. He did stop for a while, but then he started again and began inviting us to join him.

The rest of us had to make a hard decision. Would we follow Dave's invitation, or break off our friendship with him? We cared a lot about Dave—but we finally chose to stop hanging out with him, rather than jeopardize our own futures. Dave didn't even seem to mind, and he found other friends that approved of his habit.

I still wonder if there was a better way to help Dave, but that situation reminds me that friendships are often like climbing a steep trail. We can brace ourselves and lend a hand to help lift each other up, or we can relax and let others pull us down. In this case, we tried to lift Dave up, but he wasn't interested. It was a better alternative than letting him pull us down.

President Gordon B. Hinckley said, "I want to say to you, look for your friends among members of the Church. Band together and strengthen one another. And when the time of temptation comes you will have someone to lean on to bless you and give you strength when you need it. That is what this Church is for—so that we can help one another in our times of weakness to stand on our feet, tall and straight and true and good."[2]

President Kimball said, "Good company supports high morals. Oh, if our young people could learn this basic lesson to always keep good company, never to be found with those who tend to lower their standards! Let every youth select associates who will keep him on tiptoe, trying to reach the heights. Let him never choose associates who encourage him to relax in carelessness."[3]

Here is a word to parents concerning your children's friends. A little extra effort on your part can make a world of difference in the lives of your children—and their friends.

President Hinckley said, "Every boy or girl longs for friends. No one wishes to walk alone. The warmth, the comfort, the camaraderie of a friend mean everything to a boy or girl. That friend can be either an influence for good or an influence for evil. The street gangs which are so vicious are an example of friendships gone afoul.

"Conversely, the association of young people in church and their mingling in school with those of their own kind will lead them to do well and to excel in their endeavors. Open your homes to the friends of your children. If you find they have big appetites, close your eyes and let them eat. Make your children's friends your friends."[4]

Words to live by:

Spencer W. Kimball: Physical and moral safety is increased in the multiplicity of friends. Group homemade recreation activities can be not only great fun but most beneficial. Firesides may create friendships, and inspire the spirit and train the mind. Group picnics can discipline youth in gentle manners and fellowship and extend circles of intimate friends.[5]

CHAPTER 12

GAMBLING

" ... thou hast taken usury and increase,
greedily gained of thy neighbors by extortion,
and hast forgotten me, saith the Lord God.
Behold, therefore I have smitten mine hand
at thy dishonest gain which thou hast made ..."
Ezekiel 22:12-13

Gambling has become a worldwide phenomenon. If you turn on the Internet, the odds are good you will soon come across a pop-up ad inviting you to an "online casino." Not long ago, Nevada and New Jersey were the only places in the United States a person could legally gamble. But in recent years most states have relaxed their laws, and some have openly embraced gambling and lotteries as an acceptable way to raise public funding.

When a lottery jackpot reaches $100 million, people flock to buy tickets in hopes of becoming instantly rich. But when the government legalizes something that was formerly forbidden, is it now all right in the Lord's eyes?

A recent article by the Associated Press is an example of how the government is losing control of the gambling industry.

WASHINGTON — Many gambling Web sites lack adequate safeguards and warnings to prevent children and teenagers from placing illegal bets, federal regulators said Wednesday.

In a survey of 100 popular Internet gambling sites, the Federal Trade Commission found that one in five had no warnings for minors and most had disclaimers that were hard to find. The sites also lacked screening mechanisms to keep children out or had blocks that kids could easily get around.

"There is a growing problem with kids engaged in online gambling," FTC Chairman Timothy Muris said at a news conference. He said minors gambling online may use their parents' credit cards, costing them money and damaging their credit ratings.

In a warning to parents, the FTC added that online gambling can be addictive because "gambling in social isolation and using credit to gamble may be risk factors for developing gambling problems." The agency is investigating at the request of Rep. Frank Wolf, R-Va., who said the Bush administration is not doing enough to protect children from online gambling.

"Young kids are becoming addicted," Wolf said. "This Internet stuff comes right into the family room." Gambling is illegal for minors in every state, but the majority of the gambling Web sites surveyed were based outside the United States, the FTC said. The agency did not identify the sites. Wolf said the number of Internet gambling sites is climbing and the industry will probably take in about $3 billion this year.[1]

The world is now worried because of the financial consequences of gambling, but the Lord is just as worried about the spiritual consequences. President Gordon B. Hinckley said, "A lottery is a form of gambling, regardless of the high-sounding purpose it may be advocated to meet. The question of lotteries is a moral question. That government now promotes what it once enforced laws against becomes a sad reflection on the deterioration of public and political morality in the nation."[2]

The leaders of the Church have always spoken out against gambling. "From the beginning we have been advised against gambling of every sort," President Spencer W. Kimball said. "The deterioration and damage comes to the person, whether he wins or loses, to get something for nothing, something without effort, something without paying the full price."[3]

Words to live by:

Heber J. Grant: The Church has been and now is unalterably opposed to gambling in any form whatever. It is opposed to any game of chance, occupation, or so-called business, which takes money from the person who may be possessed of it without giving value received in return. It is opposed to all practices the tendency of which is to encourage the spirit of reckless speculation, and particularly to that which tends to degrade or weaken the high moral standard which members of the Church, and our community at large, have always maintained.[4]

Joseph F. Smith: The Church does not approve of gambling but strongly condemns it as morally wrong, and classes also with this gambling, games of chance and lottery, of all kinds, and earnestly disapproves of any of its members engaging therein.[5]

CHAPTER 13

GOSSIP

*Thou shalt not speak evil of thy neighbor,
nor do him any harm.*
D&C 42:27

Several years ago I worked at a daily newspaper. One day we received a story tip that seemed incredible. If it was true, it would really be newsworthy. The source said he had firsthand information that a top LDS Church leader had been spotted at a party in Salt Lake drinking alcohol and dancing on the table. Some of the editors wanted to jump on the story and put it on the front page.

Wiser heads prevailed, though, and the newspaper didn't run the story because the source was questionable. In fact, the story was soon proven to be completely false, and our newspaper would have looked ridiculous if we had published that story.

We sometimes react like those overzealous editors did. In our personal lives, we are sometimes eager to spread rumors and gossip that comes our way. It is much easier to believe such gossip when it is about someone who is just our neighbor. There may even be a thread of truth to some of the things we hear, but there is a better way, and it may even save you some embarrassment.

President Hinckley said, "Restrain your tongues in criticism of others. It is so easy to find fault. It is so much nobler to speak constructively."[1]

Brigham Young had a unique solution. He said, "If your neighbors talk about you, and you think that they do wrong in speaking evil of you, do not let them know that you ever heard a word, and conduct yourselves as if they always did right, and it will mortify them, and they will say, 'We'll not try this game any longer.'"[2]

Of course, it is possible to use gossip as a way to falsely build ourselves up at the expense of others. This is a dangerous practice, and can lead to unthinkable results.

The Prophet Joseph Smith said, "That man who rises up to condemn others, finding fault with the Church, saying that they are out of the way, while he himself is righteous, then know assuredly, that man is on the high road to apostasy; and if he does not repent, will apostatize, as God lives."[3]

Joseph F. Smith used a common phrase to describe how members of the Church should handle gossip. He said, "'*Mind your own business*' is a good motto for young people to adopt who wish to succeed, and who wish to make the best use of their time and lives. And when I say young people, it includes aged and middle-aged men and women. Let it be remembered that nothing is quite so contemptible as idle gossip."[4]

Words to live by:

Joseph F. Smith: In a letter recently received by me, the following request and question were submitted for my opinion: "I would like you to define backbiting. There seems to be a difference of opinion respecting the meaning of the term. Some claim that so long as you speak the truth about a person, it is not backbiting, no matter what you say or how you say it. Would it not be better, if we knew a person had faults, to go to him privately and labor with him, than to go to others and speak of his faults?"

President Smith's answer: Nothing could be farther from the spirit and genius of the gospel than to suppose that we are always justified in speaking the truth about a person, however harmful the truth to him may be. The gospel teaches us the fundamental principles of repentance, and we have no right to discredit a man in the estimation of his fellowmen when he has truly repented and God has forgiven him.[5]

Joseph Smith: Search yourselves—the tongue is an unruly member—hold your tongues about things of no moment—a little tale will set the world on fire.[6]

CHAPTER 14

HAPPINESS

*I would desire that ye should consider
on the blessed and happy state of those
that keep the commandments of God.
For behold, they are blessed in all things,
both temporal and spiritual; and if they
hold out faithful to the end they are received
into heaven, that thereby they may dwell
with God in a state of never-ending happiness.*
Mosiah 2:41

Today's constant materialism and "keeping up with the Joneses" is nothing new. The bigger car and spacious house won't necessarily bring happiness today, and it didn't to those in the past. The following message, given by Joseph F. Smith in the "good old days" of 1909, lets us see that the Saints nearly 100 years ago were seeking for happiness, too, and often falling into the same worldly traps.

President Smith said, "The wise man is going to steer his course away from the living death of pleasure-seeking. He is not going into bondage or debt to buy automobiles and other costly equipages to keep pace with the rush of fashionable pleasure-seeking, in this respect. He is not going to borrow money to satisfy the popular craze of traveling in Europe or in our own country, with no purpose in view but pleasure. He is not going to grow nervous and gray in a struggle for means that his wife and daughter, for mere pleasure, may spend the summer at costly, fashionable resorts, or in distant lands. It is true that there are many in our community who do not appear to be wise, and who are doing just these and other foolish acts for so-called pleasure.

"The result of this hunt for pleasure and excitement and for keeping pace with what only the very wealthy can but ought not to do, is that many are forced to undertake all kinds of illegitimate schemes to obtain money to gratify the tendency. Hence the growth of financial immorality. Many underhanded methods are adopted to obtain means, and even cheating and lying and deceiving friends and neighbors are frequently resorted to in order that money may be obtained to gratify the inordinate desire for pleasure.

"The story is told of one good lady who got flour from her grocer on credit, and sold it for cash at a bargain to get money to go pleasure-seeking. Thus the morals are corrupted. This applies to rich and poor alike.

"You men who are sensible fathers, is this course worthwhile? Young men who have a goal in sight, is this the course to take to fit your purpose and to get the best results out of life?

"Without discussing wealth and fame, shall we not call a halt in this pleasure craze, and go about the legitimate business of true Latter-day Saints, which is to desire and strive to be of some use in the world? Shall we not instead do something to increase the genuine joy and welfare and virtue of mankind as well as our own by helping to bear the burdens under which the toilers are groaning, by rendering loving, devoted and unselfish service to our fellow men?"[1]

President Gordon B. Hinckley gives great advice on how to maintain happiness in your life. He says, "Cultivate an attitude of happiness. Cultivate a spirit of optimism. Walk with faith, rejoicing in the beauties of nature, in the goodness of those you love, in the testimony which you carry in your heart concerning things divine."[2]

President Ezra Taft Benson summed it up nicely by saying, "The Lord wants us to be happy. He will do His part if we will do our part. The Christlike life is the life that brings true happiness. There is no true happiness without God."[3]

Words to live by:

David O. McKay: The first condition of happiness is a clear conscience.[4]

George Albert Smith: Our eternal happiness will be in proportion to the way that we devote ourselves to helping others.[5]

Lorenzo Snow: The thing you should have in your mind, and which you should make a motto in your life, is this: Serve God faithfully and be cheerful. The Lord has not given us the gospel that we may go around mourning all the days of our lives.[6]

CHAPTER 15

HEAVENLY PARENTS

*Furthermore we have had fathers of our flesh
which corrected us, and we gave them reverence;
shall we not much rather be in subjection
unto the Father of spirits, and live?*
Hebrews 12:9

The scripture above, written by the apostle Paul, asks a very good question. Why do we honor our earthly parents, but often turn our backs on Heavenly Father?

Of course, most people in the world today don't really understand who our Heavenly Father is. Thankfully the modern prophets have helped us gain a true understanding.

President Brigham Young said, "If we could see our Heavenly Father, we should see a being similar to our earthy parent, with this difference, our Father in Heaven is exalted and glorified. He has received his thrones, his principalities and powers, and he sits as a governor, as a monarch, and overrules kingdoms, thrones, and dominions."[1]

When the Church was organized in 1830, many of the doctrines we now know had not been revealed yet through Joseph Smith. Although Joseph had seen Heavenly Father and Jesus Christ as resurrected beings in the Sacred Grove, gospel truths were slowly revealed over the course of several years as the Saints were able to receive them.

For example, in the year 1840 Lorenzo Snow received an important personal revelation. He said, "The Spirit of the Lord rested mightily upon me—the eyes of my understanding were opened, and I saw as clear as the sun at noonday, with wonder and astonishment, the pathway of God and man. I formed the following couplet which expresses the revelation, as it was shown me:

> *As man now is, God once was:*
> *As God now is, man may be.*

President Snow continued, "I felt this to be a sacred communication, which I related to no one except my sister Eliza, until I reached England, when in a confidential private conversation with President Brigham Young, in Manchester, I related to him this extraordinary manifestation."[2]

That truly is wonderful doctrine—that Heavenly Father was once a mortal, but had progressed and become a god. And also as inspiring is that you and I—if we live righteously—can become as God now is.

Joseph Smith later shared these truths, "God himself was once as we are now, and is an exalted man, and sits enthroned in yonder heavens! That is the great secret. If the veil were rent today, and the great God who holds this world in its orbit, and who upholds all worlds and all things by his power, was to make himself visible—I say, if you were to see him today, you would see him like a man in form—like yourselves in all the person, image, and very form as a man; for Adam was created in the very fashion, image and likeness of God, and received instruction from, and walked, talked, and conversed with him, as one man talks and communes with another."[3]

Heaven is organized into family units, and when couples are sealed in Celestial marriage, they are beginning their own eternal family. By following the gospel plan, they too can become heavenly parents.

Eliza R. Snow writes the following truths in the hymn "Oh My Father":

> *"In the heav'ns are parents single?*
> *No, the thought makes reason stare!*
> *Truth is reason; truth eternal*
> *Tells me I've a mother there."*[4]

President Gordon B. Hinckley expanded on that truth. He said, "Logic and reason would certainly suggest that if we have a Father in Heaven, we have a Mother in Heaven. That doctrine rests well with me. However, in light of the instruction we have received from the Lord Himself, I regard it inappropriate for anyone in the Church to pray to our Mother in Heaven.

"The Lord Jesus Christ set the pattern in our prayers. In the Sermon on the Mount, He declared: 'After this manner therefore pray ye: Our Father which art in heaven, Hallowed be thy name.'" (3 Nephi 13:9)

President Hinckley adds, "I have looked in vain for any instance where any President of the Church, from Joseph Smith to Ezra Taft Benson, has offered a prayer to our Mother in Heaven. I suppose those who use this expression and who try to further its use are well-meaning, but they are misguided. The fact that we do not pray to our Mother in Heaven in no way belittles or denigrates her."[5]

We are literally the offspring of God, the children of heavenly parents.

Words to live by:

Joseph F. Smith: God originated and designed all things, and all (mankind) are his children. We are born into the world as his offspring; endowed with the same attributes. The children of men have sprung from the Almighty, whether the world is willing to acknowledge it or not. He is the Father of our Spirits.[6]

CHAPTER 16

HOLY GHOST

The Father has a body of flesh and bones
as tangible as man's; the Son also;
but the Holy Ghost has not a body
of flesh and bones, but is a personage of Spirit.
Were it not so, the Holy Ghost could not dwell in us.
A man may receive the Holy Ghost,
and it may descend upon him and not tarry with him.
D&C 130:22-23

The Holy Ghost is a spirit personage who plays a key role in the gospel plan. Heavenly Father hasn't revealed many details about this special person, but we do know his main duty is to testify of the truth of the gospel.

President Gordon B. Hinckley said, "The Holy Ghost stands as the third member of the Godhead, the Comforter promised by the Savior who would teach His followers all things to their remembrance, whatsoever He had said unto them. The Holy Ghost is the Testifier of Truth, who can teach men things they cannot teach one another."[1]

The *gift* of the Holy Ghost is received when someone is confirmed a member of the Church. This gift means that as long as a person is living worthily, he or she is promised to have the Holy Ghost's promptings always available.

If we listen to the promptings of the Holy Ghost—often described as "the still, small voice"—we will be warned of dangerous situations. It is our choice to listen to the promptings, or disregard them. The more we listen, the better attuned we become. If we chose to ignore the promptings, or live unrighteously, those promptings will diminish.

We all have likely ignored the promptings of the Holy Ghost at some time or another—even great men. I appreciate the humility of David O. McKay to share this story of a time he *didn't* heed the promptings of the Holy Ghost.

In the spring of 1916, President McKay was driving along the Ogden River with his brother Thomas. As they approached a small bridge that crossed the river, President McKay received a strong impression to not cross the bridge. But he ignored the prompting.

Then Thomas told him, "I think you had better not attempt to cross the bridge." But President McKay ignored his brother and stepped on the gas, only to hear Thomas say, "Oh, look out! There's a rope!"

Someone had stretched a rope across the bridge. The rope smashed the car's window, threw back the top, and hit President McKay in the chin. The rope cut open his lip, knocked out his lower teeth, and broke his upper jaw. Thomas had ducked his head and escaped unharmed. Thomas quickly took the driver's seat, turned the car around and found a doctor, who sewed President McKay's jaw into place and stitched up all his cuts.

His face was so cut up and swollen that even his friends could hardly recognize him. One of the nurses even remarked, "Too bad; he will be disfigured for life."

He received priesthood blessings, and eventually recovered with little scarring. But he had learned a great lesson—the hard way—about listening to the promptings of the Holy Ghost. [2]

Such instances were rare for David O. McKay, though.

Here is an example of when that great prophet *did* heed the promptings he received. In 1921, President McKay and Elder Hugh Cannon were making a tour of the missions of the world. After a day of inspiring conference meetings in Hilo, Hawaii, a night trip to the Kilauea volcano was arranged for the men and some of the missionaries.

They stood on the rim of that fiery pit watching the volcano, their backs chilled by the cold winds sweeping down from snowcapped Mauna Loa, while their faces were almost blistered by the heat of the molten lava. Tiring of the cold, one of the elders discovered a volcanic balcony about four feet down inside the crater where observers could watch the display without being chilled by the wind. It seemed perfectly sound, and the "railing" on the open side of it formed a fine protection from the intense heat, making it an excellent place to view the spectacular display.

After first testing its safety, President McKay and three of the elders climbed down onto the hanging balcony. As they stood there warm and comfortable, they teased the more timid ones who had hesitated to take advantage of the protection they had found.

After being down there in their protected spot for some time, President McKay suddenly said to those with him, "Brethren, I feel impressed that we should get out of here."

With that he assisted the elders to climb out, and then they in turn helped him up to the wind-swept rim. Almost immediately the whole balcony crumbled and fell with a roar into the molten lava a hundred feet or so below.

It is easy to visualize the feelings of those who witnessed this terrifying experience. Not a word was said. The only sound was the hiss and roar of the volcano.

None of those who were witnesses to that experience could ever doubt the reality of "revelation in our day." Some might say it was merely inspiration, but to them, it was a direct revelation given to a worthy man.[3]

Words to live by:

Joseph F. Smith: The one thing now that I desire to impress upon the minds of my brethren bearing the Holy Priesthood is that we should live near to the Lord, be so humble in our spirits, so tractable and pliable, under the influence of the Holy Spirit, that we will be able to know the mind and will of the Father concerning us as individuals and as officers in the Church of Christ under all circumstances.[4]

CHAPTER 17

HONESTY

And let every man deal honestly,
and be alike among this people,
and receive alike, that ye may be one,
even as I have commanded you.
D&C 51:9

The story is told of a farmer who made a trip to town each week with farm produce, which he traded to a merchant. One day after the farmer had left the store, the merchant happened to weigh a pound of the butter the farmer had just left. He was surprised to find it one ounce short. He quickly weighed the other pounds of butter and found each one to be exactly one ounce short.

When the farmer came to the store the following week, the merchant told him he was through doing business with him. He explained about his discovery of the butter, and he said that he refused to associate with any man who would stoop so low as to purposely cheat his neighbor.

The farmer removed his hat and said, "Well, we're just poor people. We don't even own a pair of scales, so in order to weigh the butter we rigged up sort of a balance. We put a one-pound bag of sugar that we buy from you on one side, and when the butter on the other side balances evenly, we figure it is a pound."

The merchant was speechless as the farmer replaced his hat and calmly walked into the store for his next order!

An incident of my youth that deeply impacted me is one my father doesn't even remember. I was eight years old and had gone with Dad to our local hardware store to buy a can of paint. We found the paint we needed, then made our purchase at the counter. We climbed back into the truck, then Dad paused to look at his receipt. "Chad, this doesn't add up. We need to go back inside."

We hopped out of the truck and marched back into the store. I figured we had been overcharged, and I was hoping maybe I could get some candy with the extra change we'd be getting back.

But to my surprise, Dad told the clerk, "You gave me too much change. The paint was $6.99, not $6.49." Then Dad pulled two quarters out of his pocket and handed it to the clerk.

At that moment, the store owner stuck his head out of an office and said to the clerk, "See, Dave? I told you Jack would be back. He's an honest man."

Dad was sheepish about it, and we went back to the truck without mentioning what had happened. But a deep impression had been made on me—the store owner considered my father "an honest man." Since that day, I have tried to follow that example.

President Gordon B. Hinckley said, "There is no substitute under the heavens for the man or woman, the boy or girl who is honest. No false words besmirch his or her reputation. No act of duplicity colors his or her conscience. He or she can walk with head high, standing above the crowd of lesser folk who constantly indulge in lying, cheating, and who excuse themselves with statements that a little lying hurts no one. It does hurt, because small lying leads to large lying, and the prisons of the nation are the best proof of that fact."[1]

In today's world, honesty is sometimes a challenge. But once you decide to be honest in all you do, you will find temptations fade away. You'll find it easier to keep your eyes on your own paper, to put in a full day's work, and so on.

If honesty hasn't been your top priority, give it a chance. You'll like it.

Words to live by:

Heber J. Grant: The fundamental thing for a Latter-day Saint is to be honest—to value his word as faithfully as his bond; to make up his mind that under no circumstances, no matter how hard it may be, by and with the help of the Lord, he will dedicate his life and his best energies to making good his promise.[2]

Joseph F. Smith: Don't do anything yourselves that you would have to say to your boy, "Don't do it." Live so that you can say, "My son, do as I do, follow me, emulate my example." That is the way fathers should live, every one of us, and it is a shame, a weakening, shameful thing for any member of the Church to pursue a course that he knows is not right, and that he would rather his children should not know.[3]

CHAPTER 18

HUMILITY

And no one can assist in this work
except he shall be humble and full of love,
having faith, hope and charity,
being temperate in all things,
whatsoever shall be entrusted to his care.
D&C 12:8

Brigham Young often said he wasn't worried about the Latter-day Saints as long as they were poor. This kept them humble. His worry was for the time when the Saints would become wealthy and forget their Heavenly Father. In some ways, that day has come.

In general, Latter-day Saints are wealthier, healthier and more talented than many of their peers. This can produce a sense of pride and superiority, unless we remember the source of our blessings. They are gifts from Heavenly Father. President Ezra Taft Benson said, "We should confess His hand in all things. Ingratitude is one of our great sins."[1]

President Hinckley said, "Be humble. Don't be arrogant. The world is full of arrogant people. Oh, how obnoxious they are! How obnoxious is an arrogant man. Girls, isn't that so? And how obnoxious, likewise, is an arrogant girl."[2]

Heber J. Grant told of an instance in his life that profoundly changed his perspective.

President Grant said, "I experienced many incidents in my youth, of wonderful inspiration and power through men preaching the gospel in the spirit of testimony and prayer. I call to mind one such incident when I was a young man, probably seventeen or eighteen years of age. I heard the late Bishop Millen Atwood preach a sermon in the Thirteenth Ward. I was studying grammar at the time, and he made some grammatical errors in his talk.

"I wrote down his first sentence, and said to myself, 'During the thirty minutes that Brother Atwood speaks, I'll get enough material to last me for the entire winter in my night school grammar class.' We had to take to the class four sentences a week that were not grammatically correct, together with our corrections.

"I contemplated making my corrections and listening to Bishop Atwood's sermon at the same time. But I did not write anything more after that first sentence—not a word; and when Millen Atwood stopped preaching, tears were rolling down my cheeks, tears of gratitude and thanksgiving that welled up in my eyes because of the marvelous testimony which that man bore of the divine mission of Joseph Smith, the prophet of God, and of the wonderful inspiration that attended the prophet in all his labors.

"Although it is now more than sixty-five years since I listened to that sermon, it is just as vivid today, and the sensations and feelings that I had are just as fixed with me as they were the day I heard it. Do you know, I would no more have thought of using those sentences in which he had made grammatical mistakes than I would think of standing up in a class and profaning the name of God. That testimony made the first profound impression that was ever made upon my heart and soul of the divine mission of the prophet. I had heard many testimonies that had pleased me and made their impression, but this was the first testimony that had melted me to tears under the inspiration of the Spirit of God to that man.

"During all the years that have passed since then, I have never been shocked or annoyed by grammatical errors or mispronounced words on the part of those preaching the gospel. I have realized that it was like judging a man by the clothes he wore, to judge the spirit of a man by the clothing of his language.

"From that day to this the one thing above all others that has impressed me has been the Spirit, the inspiration of the living God that an individual had when proclaiming the gospel, and not the language; because after all is said and done there are a great many who have never had the opportunity to become educated so far as speaking correctly is concerned. Likewise there are many who have never had an opportunity in the financial battle of life to accumulate the means whereby they could be clothed in an attractive manner. I have endeavored, from that day to this, and have been successful in my endeavor, to judge men and women by the spirit they have; for I have learned absolutely, that it is the Spirit that giveth life and understanding, and not the letter. The letter killeth."[3]

One of my most painful memories of improperly judging someone happened in fifth grade. Yes, I was young, but I also should have known better. My elementary school also served as the learning center for children in our area who had mental or physical handicaps. These children usually had their own recess time, but once in a while we overlapped. There was a young lady in that class named Gussie who had been born with serious birth defects. She had a very flat face, crooked teeth, and couldn't talk very well. Her legs were quite short, but her most obvious feature were her fingers. They were all grown together, almost like they were webbed.

During this particular recess she came toward where my friends and I were playing dodge ball. She shuffled toward me and said, "Chad, I play?"

I was surprised she knew my name, and my friends teased me a little. I acted like she hadn't said anything, so she said it again, and moved toward me on the dodge ball court. Finally I turned around and said, "Gussie, get off the court. We don't need you here." My friends added, "Yeah Gussie, get out of the way."

I watched her eyes fill with sadness. I wanted to say something nice, but I was too worried about what my friends might think. I stayed silent as her shoulders slumped and she went back into the building. As she shuffled away I had my first experience at being completely disgusted with myself—but I didn't ever have the courage to apologize to her. Gussie rarely was seen on the playground again, and when she did come out, she stayed away from me. I moved on to Middle School the next year, and I soon lost track of her.

When I was fifteen, one of my friends said he had seen Gussie's obituary in the newspaper, and that feeling of self-disgust returned. It still does at times, because I had mistreated a chosen daughter of God. Whenever I cross to the other side of the veil, one of my first objectives will be to search out Gussie and apologize for how I treated her.

However, that experience taught me a lesson, and I have tried to never again judge another person by their outward appearance. I am grateful for the functioning body I have, and I realize it is a gift. At any time it could break down or I could get in an accident. If something like that does occur, I hope people will treat me better than I treated Gussie.

I came across this poem a few years ago, and after my experience with Gussie, it really hit home.

If I look upon your twisted hands
And the braces on your feet.
If I hear the funny sounds you make
When you try to speak.
If I watch you as you try to walk
With a wobbly, weaving gait,
And see others walk away
For you, they cannot wait.
If I look upon your outer shell
And imperfections there I find,
And turn and go upon my way
The handicap is mine!
If I do not see beyond the shell
Nor look into your eyes,
To see the flame of living there
Bright and strong, Alive!
If I do not see the person
Who in that body dwells,
Who thinks and dreams and feels and hopes
And in whose heart love swells
An inner person much like me.
If this I do not find
But turn and go upon my way,
Then the handicap is mine!
—Author unknown

Words to live by:

Ezra Taft Benson: One of Satan's greatest tools is pride: to cause a man or a woman to center so much attention on self that he or she becomes insensitive to their Creator or fellow beings.[4]

Heber J. Grant: There is no danger of any man or woman losing his or her faith in this Church if he or she is humble and prayerful and obedient to duty. I have never known of such an individual losing his faith. By doing our duty, faith increases until it becomes perfect knowledge.[5]

Joseph F. Smith: We too frequently see a disposition on the part of our children to make fun of the unfortunate. A poor cripple, or a poor, weak-minded person comes along, and the boys will poke fun at him, and make unbecoming remarks about him. This is entirely wrong, and such a spirit as this should never be witnessed among the children of the Latter-day Saints.[6]

Joseph F. Smith: Let us be faithful and humble; let us live the religion of Christ, put away our follies and sins and the weaknesses of the flesh, and cleave to God and his truth with undivided hearts, and with full determination to fight the good fight of faith and continue steadfast to the end.[7]

Lorenzo Snow: The idea is not to do good because of the praise of men, but to do good because in doing good we develop godliness within us.[8]

CHAPTER 19

INTEGRITY

My lips shall not speak wickedness,
nor my tongue utter deceit. ... till I die
I will not remove mine integrity from me.
Job 27:4-5

Sometimes it is easier to explain what integrity is by showing what it is not. One day, President Spencer W. Kimball stepped into the Hotel Utah bakery in Salt Lake City to buy some hard rolls. As he placed his order, he saw a middle-aged woman he knew sitting at the counter with a cup of coffee at her plate. President Kimball was sure she saw him, though she tried not to show it. He could see her physical discomfort as she turned her face from him, and there it remained until he had made his purchase and gone his way.

President Kimball said of this experience, "She had her free agency—she could drink coffee if she wanted to, but what a wallop her character had taken, because she was unwilling to face a friend! How she shriveled! At the waters of baptism, in sacrament meetings, and in the temple, she had promised that she would have a broken heart and contrite spirit, repent of all her sins, take upon herself the name of Jesus Christ and serve him unto the end, manifesting it by her works."

He added, "Probably she was certain that I had not seen or recognized her, but the ten stories of the building above her were not enough to keep the angels in heaven from photographing her movements and recording her thoughts of deception. It was a petty thing, but for her it was withering—a weak, mean, cheap, little tricky thing that sent her honor skidding down the incline toward bankruptcy of self-esteem."[1]

It is often said we must "avoid even the appearance of evil," and that is wise counsel. President Joseph F. Smith said, "No member of the Church of Jesus Christ of Latter-day Saints can afford to do himself the dishonor, or bring upon himself the disgrace, of crossing the threshold of a liquor saloon or a gambling hall, or of any house of ill-fame of whatever name or nature it may be. No Latter-day Saint, no member of the Church, can afford it, for it is humiliating to him, it is disgraceful in him to do it, and God will judge him according to his works."[2]

President Gordon B. Hinckley took those truths one step farther. He said, "Our behavior in public must be above reproach. Our behavior in private is even more important. It must clear the standard set by the Lord. We cannot indulge in sin, let alone try to cover our sins."[3]

Words to live by:

Ezra Taft Benson: Character is the one thing we make in this world and take with us into the next.[4]

David O. McKay: The foundation of a noble character is integrity.[5]

Joseph F. Smith: You may look around today, and who are the leaders among the people but those who early and zealously devoted themselves to the faith? And you may foretell who are to be the leaders by observing the boys who show self-respect and purity and who are earnest in all good works. The Lord will not chose men from any other class of his people and exalt them into prominence. The opposite course—waiting to serve the Lord until the wild oats of youth are sown—is reprehensible. There is always something lacking in the man who spends his youth in wickedness and sin, and then turns to righteousness in later years.

Of course, the Lord honors his repentance, and it is far better that a man should turn from evil late than to continue in sin all his days, but the fact is clear that the best part of his life and strength is wasted, and there remains only poor, broken service to offer the Lord. There are regrets and heartburnings in repenting late in life from the follies and sins of youth, but there are consolations and rich rewards in serving the Lord in the vigorous days of early manhood.[6]

Brigham Young: When a man by his course in life has acquired a character that is spotless, it is a priceless jewel, and nothing should induce him to barter it away. If the wicked try to bring a blemish or cast a stain upon it, their efforts will not be successful. They may throw their mud, but it will not stain the garments of the pure and holy.[7]

CHAPTER 20

JESUS CHRIST

Behold, I am Jesus Christ the Son of God.
I created the heavens and the earth,
and all things that in them are.
3 Nephi 9:15

The Savior is often portrayed as meek and quiet—which he was at times. But those portrayals often leave the impression he was weak—which he certainly wasn't!

One of the more eloquent descriptions of the Savior's personality is found in the excellent work *Jesus the Christ* by Elder James E. Talmage. While discussing the Savior's cleansing of the temple, Elder Talmage writes:

"The incident of Christ's forcible clearing of the temple is a contradiction of the traditional conception of Him as of One so gentle and unassertive in demeanor as to appear unmanly. Gentle He was, and patient under affliction, merciful and long-suffering in dealing with contrite sinners, yet stern and inflexible in the presence of hypocrisy, and unsparing in His denunciation of persistent evil-doers. His mood was adapted to the conditions to which He addressed Himself; tender words of encouragement or burning expletives of righteous indignation issued with equal fluency from His lips. His nature was no poetic conception of cherubic sweetness ever present, but that of a Man, with the emotions and passions essential to manhood and manliness. He, who often wept with compassion, at other times evinced in word and action the righteous anger of a God. But of all His passions, however gently they rippled or strongly surged, He was ever master. Contrast the gentle Jesus moved to hospitable service by the needs of a festal party in Cana (turning water into wine), with the indignant Christ plying His whip, and amidst commotion and turmoil of His own making, driving cattle and men before Him as an unclean herd."[1]

I love that description, because it gives a glimpse into the true nature of the Savior, the person who atoned for our sins, and who will stand as our judge before Heavenly Father. The more we come to know the Savior, the closer to heaven we will be.

After receiving word of President Wilford Woodruff's death, President Lorenzo Snow knew the mantle of the presidency was now upon him. He went to the Salt Lake Temple, where he pleaded with the Lord to reveal His divine will.

Upon concluding his prayer he waited for an immediate answer, but none seemed to be forthcoming. Some time later his granddaughter Allie Young Pond gave the following account of what happened later that night.

She said, "One evening while I was visiting Grandpa Snow in his room in the Salt Lake Temple, I remained until the door-keepers had gone and the night-watchmen had not yet come in, so Grandpa said he would take me to the main front entrance and let me out that way. He got his bunch of keys from his dresser. After we left his room and while we were still in the large corridor leading into the Celestial Room, I was walking several steps ahead of Grandpa when he stopped me and said, 'Wait a moment, Allie, I want to tell you something. It was right here that the Lord Jesus Christ appeared to me at the time of the death of President Woodruff. He instructed me to go right ahead and reorganize the First Presidency of the Church at once and not wait as had been done after the death of the previous presidents, and that I was to succeed President Woodruff.'

"Then Grandpa came a step nearer, held out his left hand and said, 'He stood right here, about three feet above the floor. It looked as though He stood on a plate of solid gold.'

"Grandpa told me what a glorious personage the Savior is and described His hands, feet, countenance and beautiful white robes, all of which were of such a glory of whiteness and brightness that he could hardly gaze upon Him."[2]

President David O. McKay had an experience that showed him the future home of those who follow the Savior. President McKay beheld in vision a beautiful white city. He said, "I seemed to realize that trees with luscious fruit, shrubbery with gorgeously-tinted leaves, and flowers in perfect bloom abounded everywhere. The clear sky above seemed to reflect these beautiful shades of color. I then saw a great concourse of people approaching the city. Each one wore a white flowing robe, and a white headdress. Instantly the attention seemed centered upon their leader, and though I could see only the profile of his features and his body, I recognized him at once as my Savior! The tint and radiance of his countenance were glorious to behold! There was peace about him which seemed sublime—it was divine!

"The city, I understood, was his. It was the City Eternal; and the people following him were to abide there in peace and eternal happiness.

"But who were they? As if the Savior read my thoughts, he answered by pointing to a semicircle that then appeared above them, and on which were written in gold the words: *'These Are They Who Have Overcome The World—Who Have Truly Been Born Again!'*"[3]

Words to live by:

Gordon B. Hinckley: Jesus Christ is the key figure of our faith. The official name of the Church is The Church of Jesus Christ of Latter-day Saints. We worship him as Lord and Savior.[4]

Ezra Taft Benson: The only true test of greatness, blessedness, and joyfulness is how close a life can come to being like the Master, Jesus Christ. He is the right way, the full truth, and the abundant life.[5]

Spencer W. Kimball: We all need heroes to honor and admire; we need people after whom we can pattern our lives. For us Christ is the chiefest of these.[6]

Joseph Fielding Smith: The Savior bought us with his blood. We belong to him, whether we know it or not; everybody does. He has a right to tell us what to do; he has a right to punish when we violate the laws he has given; he has the right to reward when we are obedient.[7]

Heber J. Grant: Not only did Jesus come as a universal gift, He came as an individual offering with a personal message to each one of us. For each one of us He died on Calvary and His blood will conditionally save us. Not as nations, communities or groups, but as individuals.[8]

Joseph F. Smith: The grand object of our coming to this earth is that we may become like Christ, for if we are not like him, we cannot become the sons of God, and be joint heirs with Christ.[9]

Wilford Woodruff: No man ever did or ever will obtain salvation, only through the ordinances of the gospel and through the name of Jesus. There can be no change in the gospel; all men that are saved from Adam to infinitum are saved by the one system of salvation.[10]

Brigham Young: The greatest and most important of all requirements of our Father in Heaven is to believe in Jesus Christ, confess him, seek him, cling to him, make friends with him. Take a course to open a communication with your Elder Brother.[11]

CHAPTER 21

MISSIONARY SERVICE

*Wherefore, you are called to cry repentance
unto this people. And if it so be that you should labor
all your days in crying repentance unto this people,
and bring, save it be one soul unto me,
how great shall be your joy with him
in the kingdom of my Father!
And now, if your joy will be great with one soul
that you have brought unto me
into the kingdom of my Father,
how great will be your joy
if you should bring many souls unto me!*
D&C 18:14-16

Few things we do in life carry on for generations, but missionary work is one that does. Sharing the gospel is like throwing a pebble into a pond and watching the ripples expand across the water. The people you teach the gospel to will then share it with others, and it will spread like those ripples in the pond.

Sometimes the hardest part of a mission is actually getting out there. President Heber C. Kimball and Brigham Young left for their missions to Great Britain under the most difficult of circumstances. Both they and their families were very ill, but they were determined to fulfill their missions no matter what.

Elder Kimball described their departure: "I went to

my bed and shook hands with my wife Vilate who was then shaking with a chill, having two children lying sick by her side; I embraced her and my children, and bade them farewell. My only well child was little Heber P., and it was with difficulty he could carry a couple of quarts of water at a time, to assist in quenching their thirst.

"It was with difficulty we got into the wagon, and started down the hill about ten rods; it appeared to me as though my very inmost parts would melt within me at leaving my family in such a condition, as it were almost in the arms of death. I felt as though I not could endure it. I asked the teamster to stop, and said to Brother Brigham, 'This is pretty tough, isn't it; let's rise up and give them a cheer.' We arose, and swinging our hats three times over our heads, shouted, 'Hurrah, Hurrah for Israel.'

"Vilate, upon earing the noise, arose from her bed and came to the door. She had a smile on her face. Vilate and Mary Ann Young cried out to us: 'Good-bye, God bless you.' We returned the compliment, and then told the driver to go ahead. After this I felt a spirit of joy and gratitude, having had the satisfaction of seeing my wife standing upon her feet, instead of leaving her in bed, knowing well that I should not see them again for two or three years."[1]

In the following years those two brethren converted hundreds of people to the Church in Great Britain. What if they had decided to let family concerns keep them home?

I served a mission among the Spanish-speaking people of New Jersey, a place I had never really even thought of before I opened my mission call, but I believe I was sent there to take the gospel to certain people.

The most forceful incident that told me I was serving where I should came while knocking on doors. I had a new companion straight from the Missionary Training Center, Elder Marty Hepworth from Orderville, Utah. He was really fired up about missionary work, and we spent several hours each day knocking on doors. We decided to work in a rundown part of the city where missionaries hadn't tracted in at least a year.

In one apartment building, a teenage girl answered the door. We explained who we were, and she told us to come back that evening, because her mom was interested in religion.

We returned that night, and the same girl opened the door and invited us in. At that moment, her mother came into the room. The lady's face went white and she put her hand to her mouth. Then she tried to say something, but couldn't get the words out. Elder Hepworth and I just looked at each other, unsure what was happening.

The lady went back into the kitchen, got a drink and finally returned. Nothing more was said about her reaction, and we taught the family, including her husband, the first discussion. The lady, Ana Jimenez, seemed to absorb every word we said.

The next night, we taught the family the second discussion, then I asked Ana if she would consider being baptized. She immediately said, "Yes."

Then she smiled and asked if we were curious about her reaction the previous day. We nodded, and she told us the following story.

She said, "I have been seeking God's true church for many years, but for the past six months I have been praying very hard that the truth would be shown to me. Then about three months ago I had a very vivid dream. Two young American men came to my home. They were wearing white shirts and ties, and each one was carrying a backpack. A voice in my dream said these messengers would bring me the truth. In the dream, I saw the faces of these men, and they are the same faces I am looking at right now! You are the messengers I saw!"

We were stunned to hear Ana's words, and humbled that we had fulfilled her dream. As we talked about it later that night, we realized Ana had received her dream even before Elder Hepworth had entered the MTC. What if he had changed his mind at the last minute?

Since we were tracting in a part of the city where missionaries seldom went, the odds are slim that Ana and her family would have heard the gospel message for a long time, if ever.

What a missed opportunity that would have been. After her baptism, Ana became a referral machine, giving us names of several people to teach. When I ended my mission the following year, she had brought ten of her friends into the church, and has since brought many more.

In other words, if you are preparing for a mission, there will likely be a time in the future when *you* need to be the one knocking on that specific door in some distant city, starting the "ripple effect" in your own life. What can compare? A new car? A girlfriend? Finishing college a little sooner? The positive spiritual experiences of a mission far outweigh anything postponed or left at home.

On the flip side, we have these words from President Spencer W. Kimball, who said, "If we do not do our duty in regard to missionary service, then I am convinced that God will hold us responsible for the people we might have saved had we done our duty."[2]

Since missionary service is such a vital turning point in the lives of young people, Satan will do all he can to entice them to stay home.

President Gordon B. Hinckley said, "I know that our young men are under a great obligation to qualify themselves through education to fill positions of responsibility in the world. Their time is precious. But I do not hesitate to promise that the time spent in faithful and devoted service as a missionary declaring the Master will only add to their qualifications for positions of responsibility in the future.

"Regardless of the vocation they choose to pursue, they will be better qualified in their powers of expression, in their habits of industry, in the value they place on training, in the integrity of their lives, and in their recognition of a higher source of strength and power than that which lies within their native capacity."[3]

In another address, President Hinckley emphasized that a mission not only helps the missionary, but also helps the Lord accomplish His purposes. He said, "I hope that every young man has a mission on his list of goals. I hope that you will not let anything get in the way of that. The Lord needs you. He needs your help. He needs your strength. He needs your voice. We are all the Lord has to do His work, and we must work at it and work together to accomplish His divine purposes."[4]

Words to live by:

Spencer W. Kimball: Every LDS male who is worthy and able should fill a mission.[5]

George Albert Smith: Begin on the man who lives next door by inspiring confidence in him, by inspiring love in him for you because of your righteousness, and your missionary work has already begun.[6]

Joseph F. Smith: Concerning missionaries, we do not want boys that have been in saloons, that have been in houses of ill-fame, that have been gamblers, that have been drunkards, that have been infamous in their lives—we do not want such to go into the ministry of this holy gospel to represent the Son of the living God and the power of redemption to the world. We want young men who have been born or adopted in the covenant, who have been reared in purity, who have kept themselves unspotted from the world, and can go into the nations of the earth and say to men, "Follow me, as I follow Christ."[7]

Wilford Woodruff: Get the Spirit of God before you go on your missions or anywhere else. Get the spirit of revelation with you. When you get that you are safe, and you will do exactly what the Lord wants you to do.[8]

CHAPTER 22

MODESTY and FASHION STYLES

... there began to be among them
those who were lifted up in pride,
such as the wearing of costly apparel,
and all manner of fine pearls,
and of the fine things of the world.
4 Nephi 1:24

One of my friends, Dusty, shared with our priesthood quorum a major dilemma. We could all relate to the uncomfortable situation he faced.

Dusty has a teenage sister-in-law. During a family party at a park, she was wearing a sleeveless shirt and small, tight shorts. Dusty saw a young man staring at her, and he felt he should tell her that by showing that much of her body, she could give the wrong impression to boys.

Dusty told her, "I know you aren't having bad thoughts when you wear those clothes, but it can cause boys to make you the subject of their bad thoughts. You can help boys control their thoughts by dressing more modestly." She thanked him, saying she hadn't even realized her outfit could be giving the wrong signal.

Dusty told us, "Believe me, it was not an easy thing to tell a righteous daughter of God that by wearing that outfit she was causing bad thoughts in the minds of other people. It was a real eye-opener to her, and I think many girls don't realize how distracting their clothing—or lack of clothing—can be."

The same can be said for swimsuits, especially bikinis. Modesty should be a top consideration. Young men respect modesty far more than they would have you believe.

Can you guess what year a modern prophet made the following statement?

"In my sight the present-day fashions are abominable, suggestive of evil, calculated to arouse base passion and lust, and to engender lasciviousness, in the hearts of those who follow the fashions, and of those who tolerate them. Why? Because women are imitating the very customs of a class of women who have resorted to that means to aid them to sell their souls. It is infamous, and I hope the daughters of Zion will not descend to these pernicious ways, customs and fashions, for they are demoralizing and damnable in their effect."[1]

Was that in 1988? 1968? Try 1918. Joseph F. Smith had noticed a downward trend in fashion even then. Who knows what he would say about today's midriff-baring, low-cut tops and tight, hip-hugging jeans!

Guidelines for young women

President Spencer W. Kimball served in the Quorum of the Twelve during the 1960s, when teenage fashions such as the miniskirt really became an issue. He didn't like speaking out on such things, but he knew it was his duty. His words are as timely now as they were then.

He said, "You girls go and find modest clothes and wear them. Make them as beautiful as you can and be attractive. Make up to your boyfriends in bright intellect and sweet spirit and attractive demeanor that which some girls can only do with their bodies.

"It is a pretty weak girl if she has only her body to attract somebody. . . You can always be in style and still be modest. I have never seen a style yet in my many years that one couldn't follow and still be modest. Our girls don't need to be backwoods, neither do they need to dress like a harlot. There is a nice medium place where everybody can dress well.

"When dresses are long, you can wear them long; and when they are flaring, you can wear them flaring; and when they are short, you can wear them short; but you don't need to outdo everybody in getting them short.

"If you want to stay in the realm of modest womanhood, you keep your body covered and no decent man will ever think less of you for it and every good, honorable man who would think of marrying you would love you more for it. There is no time when a Latter-day Saint woman should wear a strapless gown. They are not righteous nor approved."[2]

President Kimball gave wise advice on another issue. He said, "Boys seldom criticize a girl for using too little makeup. Sometimes they say, 'She's a nice girl, but she uses too much makeup.' To be overdressed, to be gaudily dressed, to be dressed to look sexy, to be overdecorated is bad taste, to say the least. The young woman is smart who can don just enough powder and lipstick to convince the fellows it isn't makeup at all, but the 'real' you."[2]

Guidelines for young men

Don't worry, President Kimball didn't let the young men off the hook. He said, "Sometimes we have young men, they swim scantily clad, of course, when they are in the water—that's all right. Sometimes they play games, basketball, for instance, with very, very little on them. Maybe that's all right on the basketball floor, but certainly it is immodest for them to go around dating before and after the game in those kinds of clothes. It is just as bad for a man to be undressed as it is for a woman to be undressed and that, I am sure, is the gospel of Christ. We have only one standard of morality, only one standard of decency, only one standard of modesty, and I hope our men will remember that. There is no reason why a man should go around half-dressed, either, before the people."[3]

President Kimball also said, "Young men should keep their faces shaved, their hair combed, their haircuts reasonably conservative, their nails cleaned. Overtight, suggestive pants brand young men as vulgar. Young people can be smart and personable, dignified and attractive by finding an area somewhere less than the extremes and still be in good style."[4]

Piercing

Some fads are harmless fun and go away quickly. The fad of body piercing, though, certainly isn't harmless. This includes the piercing of the body for multiple rings in the ears, in the nose, in the belly button—even stainless-steel rods through the tongue. Concerning such piercings, President Hinckley said, "Can they possibly think that is beautiful? It is a passing fancy, but its effects can be permanent. Some have gone to such extremes that the ring had to be removed by surgery. The First Presidency and the Quorum of the Twelve have declared that we discourage tattoos and also 'the piercing of the body for other than medical purposes.' We do not, however, take any position 'on the minimal piercing of the ears by women for one pair of earrings'—one pair."[5]

Tattoos

When my grandfather joined the Navy in the 1940s, he did what many new sailors did—he got a tattoo of an anchor on his arm. He did it for a noble purpose—to show patriotism. But now, at 80 years old, he still has that tattoo "anchored" to his arm. He once told me he wished he had never gotten it.

At least Grandpa's tattoo had a logical purpose. I feel sad when I see a handsome young man who has a strange design tattooed on his neck or back. Maybe he put it there so he can't see it—but the rest of the world can. Most people are saying to themselves, "What was he thinking?"

President Hinckley put it well in a recent address concerning tattoos. He said, "I cannot understand why any young man—or young woman, for that matter—would wish to undergo the painful process of disfiguring the skin with various multicolored representations of people, animals, and various symbols. With tattoos, the process is permanent, unless there is another painful and costly undertaking to remove it. Fathers, caution your sons against having their bodies tattooed. They may resist your talk now, but the time will come when they will thank you. A tattoo is graffiti on the temple of the body."[6]

Words to live by:

David O. McKay: A beautiful, modest, gracious woman is creation's masterpiece.[8]

Brigham Young: This is my scripture: They who long and lust after the fashions of the world are destitute of the Spirit of God.[9]

CHAPTER 23

MUSIC

And it shall be given thee, also, to make a selection
of sacred hymns, as it shall be given thee,
which is pleasing unto me, to be had in my church.
For my soul delighted in the song of the heart;
yea, the song of the righteous is a prayer unto me,
and it shall be answered
with a blessing upon their heads.
D&C 25: 11-12

In 1830, soon after the Church was organized, Emma Smith was commanded by the Lord in the scripture listed above to compile hymns that the members could use in worship services. Since that time, music has been an essential part of our meetings.

A great number of Latter-day Saints are talented musicians. Every ward is filled with wonderful pianists and singers. These talented performers share their music in many ways, through church performances or public events.

Over the years, many LDS musicians have reached a national audience, most notably the various members of the Osmond family. The Wolfgramm family, also known as the Jets, had many hit songs. Recently, the musical trio SHeDAISY, composed of the Osborn sisters from Magna, Utah, have made a big impact in country music.

These performers and other LDS music artists are

playing a role in spreading good, uplifting music to the world. There are also many groups within the LDS culture whose music is powerful and soothing.

President Gordon B. Hinckley said, "We recognize the universal power of music to touch the hearts of men and women everywhere and in all generations—to inspire and encourage, to sustain and lift, to comfort and bring peace."[1]

Yes, music is a wonderful thing. It can bring us out of a bad mood and cause us to dance across the room. Even now—long past our teenage years—when my brothers and I get together, music is a main topic we discuss.

Naturally, there are pitfalls in the music world. Many times a popular artist might have a wonderful song, but the rest of the CD will essentially be trash.

During high school, I bought a cassette tape of one of the most popular singers of the 1980s. His songs were always on the radio, and were played at our school dances. But when I bought his tape, I sadly realized the songs that weren't being played on the radio were filthy. The melodies were quite good, but the words made me very uncomfortable.

I went to my dad's tool chest, grabbed a hammer, and with one solid blow I smashed that tape to pieces. I missed hearing the songs I liked, but it wasn't worth having to fast forward through the ones I didn't like.

CDs make it easier to skip over the songs that aren't uplifting, but you must choose if it is worth having such music in your home.

President Hinckley suggests another alternative. "Enjoy music. Not the kind that rocks and rolls, but the music of the masters, the music that has lived through the centuries, the music that has lifted people. If you do not have a taste for it, listen to it thoughtfully. If you do not like it the first time, listen to it again and keep listening. It will be something like going to the temple. The more often you go, the more beautiful will be the experience."[2]

Hymns can cleanse your mind—and lift the spirit. The Church sells a 14-CD set of all the hymns in the hymnbook for just $9.50 (plus shipping). The set is available from the Church Distribution Center or at **www.ldscatalog.com.**

You might consider adding the hymns to your CD collection—and really freak out your parents! Besides, you might find yourself popping it into your CD player more often than you would have thought.

Words to live by:

Ezra Taft Benson: We encourage you to listen to uplifting music, both popular and classical, that builds the spirit. Learn some favorite hymns from our hymnbook that build faith and spirituality. Attend dances where the music and the lighting and the dance movements are conducive to the Spirit.[3]

Joseph F. Smith: When young men go out into the world to preach the gospel, they will find it very beneficial for them to know how to sing the songs of Zion. I repeat the admonition of Brother McMurrin, who has recently returned from a lengthy mission to Europe, that the young men who are eligible to preach the gospel, and that are likely to be called into the missionary field, begin at once to improve their talent to sing, and do not think it is beneath their dignity to join the choirs of the wards in which they live and learn how to sing.[4]

CHAPTER 24

PATRIARCHAL BLESSINGS

... my servant Hyrum may take the office
of Priesthood and Patriarch, which was appointed
unto him by his father, by blessing and also by right;
That from henceforth he shall hold the keys of the
patriarchal blessing upon the heads of all my people,
that whoever he blesses shall be blessed,
and whoever he curses shall be cursed;
that whatsoever he shall bind on earth
shall be bound in heaven.
D&C 124: 91-93

Have you ever wished you could take a peek into your future? Wouldn't it make such a difference in how you live your daily life?

In a very real sense, that great opportunity is possible for you. Heavenly Father has provided a way—through a patriarchal blessing.

A patriarchal blessing allows you to gain a sense of what lies ahead for you, and what the Lord expects of you.

President Ezra Taft Benson said, "I would encourage you to receive a patriarchal blessing. Study it carefully and regard it as personal scripture to you—for that indeed is what it is."[1]

Church members should receive a patriarchal blessing as soon as they are spiritually ready, which is often during their early teenage years. I received my patriarchal blessing at age 14, and it played a major role in how I lived my life during my teenage years—and beyond.

Of his own patriarchal blessing, President Gordon B. Hinckley said, "I count my patriarchal blessing as one of the great sacred things of my life. A patriarchal blessing is a unique and sacred and personal and wonderful thing that may be given to every member of this Church who lives worthy of it."[2]

When you receive your patriarchal blessing, it might take time—even years—before certain parts become clear to you. It may even indicate things that seem impossible. But remember, all things are possible through the Lord.

One day during my mission my companion Elder Trent Price received a letter from his cousin. The cousin said he had just received his patriarchal blessing, and it said he would serve a mission among the people in Russia.

This was in 1988, and Elder Price's cousin was sixteen. The Berlin Wall was still solidly in place, and the Soviet Union appeared as strong as ever—and as opposed to missionary work as ever.

I was admittedly skeptical. "Are you saying that within three years he'll be serving in Russia? That just doesn't seem possible."

Elder Price shrugged and said, "That's what his blessing said."

I tucked our conversation into the back of my mind, and then watched in the following years as Communism collapsed and LDS missionaries began serving in the former Soviet Union, particularly Russia.

In 1991 I saw Elder Price again when we crossed paths in a class at BYU. I asked him if his cousin had ended up on a mission in Russia.

Elder Price smiled and said, "He's there right now!"

If you feel a desire to receive your patriarchal blessing, don't hesitate. A patriarchal blessing is a special gift from Heavenly Father. Once you receive it, live your life so that those promised blessings will be fulfilled.

Some people feel they must wait until the bishop approaches them about it. This isn't so. Let your bishop know you would like a patriarchal blessing. He will interview you and help you arrange an appointment with your stake patriarch.

Go for it!

Words to live by:

David O. McKay: Patriarchal blessings contemplate an inspired declaration of the lineage of the recipient, and also where so moved upon by the Spirit, an inspired and prophetic statement of the life mission of the recipient, together with such blessings, cautions, and admonitions as the patriarch may be prompted to give for the accomplishment of such life's mission. It is always made clear that the realization of the promised blessings is conditioned upon faithfulness to the gospel of our Lord, whose servant the patriarch is. All such blessings are recorded and generally only one such blessing should be adequate for each person's life.[3]

CHAPTER 25

PRAYER

*But behold, I say unto you that ye must pray always,
and not faint; that ye must not perform any thing
unto the Lord save in the first place
ye shall pray unto the Father in the name of Christ,
that he will consecrate thy performance unto thee,
that thy performance may be
for the welfare of thy soul.*
2 Nephi 32:9

Do you ever go a whole day without talking to your parents? If you do, don't you feel a bit empty inside? In the same way, we can develop an empty feeling if we fail to talk to Heavenly Father on a regular basis.

The scripture above says we should "pray always." What that means is to develop the habit of praying in your heart in your daily life. When you take a test in school or get ready for an important basketball game, do you ever pray in your mind for help to do your best?

That is what Nephi is saying in the above scripture. He says if we include Heavenly Father in all our activities, the Lord will be our guide, and bless us. And naturally, the types of activities we do will be more uplifting and pure.

Our prophets have always emphasized the importance of prayer. President Gordon B. Hinckley said there is no other resource to compare with prayer. He added, "To think that each of us may approach our Father in Heaven, who is the great God of the universe, for individual help and guidance, for strength and faith, is a miracle in and of itself. We come to Him by invitation. Let us not shun the opportunity which He has afforded us."[1]

Personal prayer

When we pray, it is like sending a phone call to Heavenly Father. But like any parent, He would prefer that your "calls" to Him are more than distress calls. President Howard W. Hunter said, "If prayer is only a spasmodic cry at the time of crisis, then it is utterly selfish, and we come to think of God as a repairman or a service agency to help us only in our emergencies."[2]

Instead, it should be a two-way conversation. If we sincerely do our part, Heavenly Father will answer us. President Spencer W. Kimball gave this advice, "At the end of our prayers, we need to do some intense listening—even for several minutes. Sometimes ideas flood our mind as we listen after our prayers. Sometimes feelings press upon us. A spirit of calmness assures us that all will be well. But always, if we have been honest and earnest, we will experience a good feeling—a feeling of warmth from our Father in Heaven and a sense of his love for us."[3]

President Gordon B. Hinckley gives these powerful words: "You never need be ashamed of praying. Get on your knees as the day starts. Get on your knees as the day closes and offer prayer unto the Lord, and ask Him to bless you in dealing with your problems, to bless you in your schooling, bless you in all you do, and remember before Him those who are less fortunate than you, others who are in trouble and need and desire His blessings. Be prayerful!"[4]

Family prayer

The power that comes from gathering the family together for prayer has long been known to the modern prophets. President Heber J. Grant said, "I am convinced that one of the greatest things that can come into any home to cause the boys and girls in that home to grow up in a love of God and in a love of the gospel of Jesus Christ is to have family prayer; not for the father of the family alone to pray, but for the mother and for the children to do so also, that they may partake of the spirit of prayer."[5]

Family prayer also helps both parents and children remember how truly blessed they are. President Spencer W. Kimball said, "Pray in thanksgiving. In many countries, the homes are barren and the cupboards bare—no books, no radios, no pictures, no furniture, no fire—while we are housed adequately, clothed warmly, fed extravagantly. Did we show our thanks by proper devotion on our knees last night and this morning?"[6]

If family prayer hasn't been part of your family's life, it might not hurt to be the one to suggest it does.

Words to live by:

Heber J. Grant: When men stop praying for God's Spirit, they place confidence in their own unaided reason, and they gradually lose the Spirit of God, just the same as near and dear friends, by never writing to or visiting with each other, will become strangers.[7]

Joseph F. Smith: It is not such a difficult thing to learn how to pray. It is not the words we use particularly that constitute prayer. Prayer does not consist of words, altogether. True, faithful, earnest prayer consists more in the feelings that rises from the heart and from the inward desire of our spirits to supplicate the Lord in humility and in faith, that we may receive his blessings. It matters not how simple the words may be, if our desires are genuine and we come before the Lord with a broken heart and a contrite spirit to ask him for that which we need.[8]

Wilford Woodruff: Never proceed to do anything until you go and labor in prayer and get the Holy Spirit. Wherever the Spirit dictates you to go or to do, that will be right; and, by following its dictates, you will come out all right.[9]

John Taylor: I am reminded of my boyhood. At that early period of my life I learned to approach God. Many a time I have gone into the fields and concealing myself behind some bush, would bow before the Lord and call upon him to guide and direct me. And he heard my prayer.[10]

Brigham Young: When you get up in the morning, before you suffer yourselves to eat one mouthful of food, call your wife and children together, bow down before the Lord, ask him to forgive your sins, and protect you through the day, to preserve you from temptation and all evil, to guide your steps aright, that you may do something that day that shall be beneficial to the kingdom of God on the earth. Have you time to do this? Elders, sisters, have you time to pray?[11]

CHAPTER 26

SCRIPTURE STUDY

And the Book of Mormon and the holy scriptures
are given of me for your instruction;
and the power of my Spirit quickened all things.
D&C 33:16

The LDS Church recognizes four distinct books as holy scripture—The Bible, The Book of Mormon, The Doctrine and Covenants, and The Pearl of Great Price. There are many other wonderful, helpful books in the world, but how many contain the actual words of Jesus Christ?

There have been several movies made about men chasing a marvelous treasure across the globe, sacrificing nearly everything to gain that treasured possession. What if the evening news told the world that heavenly messengers had revealed the location of an ancient record that contained clear, precise instructions on how to live forever in Celestial glory? Don't you think people everywhere would be eager to know what the record said?

That *has* happened in our day. The location of ancient gold plates was revealed to Joseph Smith by Moroni, a resurrected Nephite prophet. Through the power of God, Joseph translated the plates into the Book of Mormon, and those words are now flooding the earth.

Joseph Smith said, "I told the brethren that the Book of Mormon was the most correct of any book on earth, and the keystone of our religion, and a man would get nearer to God by abiding by its precepts, than by any other book."[1]

Despite having this marvelous record in our homes, the precious message is often ignored. If we allow it to happen, daily activities will crowd out time for scripture study. Here is a humorous little poem that carries much truth:

Cherished Literature

One is well-worn and cherished with pride;
Not the Book of Mormon, but the TV Guide.
One is used daily to help folks decide;
Nope, not the Book of Mormon, but the TV Guide.

As pages are turned, what shall they see?
Oh, what does it matter? Turn on the TV.
So they open the book from which they confide;
No, not the Book of Mormon, but the TV Guide.

In their home, the Word of God is seldom read;
Maybe a verse or two before they fall into bed.
The family is exhausted and as sleepy as can be,
Not from reading scriptures, but from watching TV.

In your home, which book is well-read,
and which one gathers dust?
Your answer may show whether you've gained
the Lord's trust.
The Lord's gospel plan is given for all to see,
But it is found in the scriptures, not on TV.

—*Author Unknown*

The scriptures are provided to help us stay in tune with Heavenly Father. Church leaders have often asked us to read daily from the scriptures, for even as little as ten minutes a day. This can have a profound positive effect on our lives. President Spencer W. Kimball said, "I find when I get casual in my relationships with divinity and when it seems that no divine ear is listening and no divine voice is speaking, that I am far, far away. If I immerse myself in the scriptures, the distance narrows and the spirituality returns."[2]

Possibly the greatest benefit of scripture reading is the spiritual strength that comes to those who read daily. President Ezra Taft Benson said, "The Book of Mormon will change your life. It will fortify you against the evils of our day. It will bring a spirituality into your life that no other book will. It will be the most important book you will read in preparation for a mission and for life.

"A young man who knows and loves the Book of Mormon, who has read it several times, who has an abiding testimony of its truthfulness, and who applies its teachings will be able to stand against the wiles of the devil and will be a mighty tool in the hands of the Lord."[3]

President Benson also said, "I have noted within the Church the difference in discernment, in insight, conviction and spirit between those who know and love the Book of Mormon and those who do not. That book is a great sifter."[4]

If you don't have your own set of scriptures, ask your parents or bishop if you could receive a set. President Spencer W. Kimball said, "We have recommended that so far as possible all the children have their own scriptures and learn to use them."[5]

Words to live by:

Joseph Fielding Smith: No member of the Church can stand approved in the presence of God who has not seriously and carefully read the Book of Mormon. [6]

George Albert Smith: I admonish you, O Israel, search the Scriptures; read them in your homes; teach your families what the Lord has said; let us spend less of our time reading the unimportant and often harmful literature of the day and go to the fountain of truth and read the word of the Lord.[7]

Joseph F. Smith: The book of Doctrine and Covenants contains some of the most glorious principles ever revealed to the world, some that have been revealed in greater fulness than they were ever revealed before to the world; and this, in fulfillment of the promise of the ancient prophets that in the latter times the Lord would reveal things to the world that had been kept hidden from the foundation thereof; and the Lord has revealed them through the Prophet Joseph Smith.[8]

Wilford Woodruff: The Bible, the Book of Mormon, and the Doctrine and Covenants contain the words of eternal life unto this generation, and they will rise in judgment against those who reject them.[9]

Brigham Young: The book of Doctrine and Covenants is given for the Latter-day Saints expressly for their everyday walk and actions.[10]

CHAPTER 27

SEXUAL PURITY

*And this is not all, my son. Thou didst do that which
was grievous unto me; for thou didst forsake the
ministry, and did go over into the land of Siron
among the borders of the Lamanites, after the harlot
Isabel. Yea, she did steal away the hearts of many;
but this was no excuse for thee, my son. ... Know ye
not that these things are an abomination in the sight
of the Lord; yea, most abominable above all sins
save it be the shedding of innocent blood
or denying the Holy Ghost?*
Alma 39: 3-5

The above scripture contains the anguished words of
the prophet Alma the Younger to his son Corianton, who
had spent time with a harlot and violated the law of
chastity. Alma makes plain the importance of sexual
purity in the eyes of the Lord, placing sexual sin behind
only murder and forsaking the Holy Ghost.

No wonder Satan is doing all he can to lead people into
the serious trap of sexual relations before marriage.
Repentance is possible, but is a long, painful road.
Chastity is the Lord's way—remaining virtuous and
morally pure. A person breaks the law of chastity by taking
part in sexual activities outside the bonds of marriage.
There are varying forms and degrees of unchastity, and
they will be discussed in this chapter.

President Gordon B. Hinckley said, "We believe in

chastity before marriage and total fidelity after marriage. That sums it up. That is the way to happiness in living. That is the way to satisfaction. It brings peace to the heart and peace to the home."[1]

A poem from the 1700s still applies to how we allow sin to creep into our lives.

Vice is a monster of so frightful mien,
As to be hated, needs but to be seen;
Yet seen too oft,
Familiar with her face,
We first endure, then pity, then embrace.
—Alexander Pope

As the poem says, when we first encounter "vice"—or evil—we hate it immediately. But if we let it hang around and become familiar with it, we first endure it, then find ourselves sympathetic toward it, then finally embrace it.

Isn't that evident in the world's definition of right and wrong today? It has taken Satan many years of gradual introduction of sexual themes into the popular culture, but now he has modern society on a slippery slope that will be very difficult to ever climb back up.

From all indications, the world's values will continue down that slope. But that doesn't mean Latter-day Saints must follow that path. In fact, if we are to live again with our Heavenly Father, we *must* choose a different path altogether—righteousness.

President Hinckley has said, "There is no peace to be had through sexual impurity. Our Heavenly Father placed within us the desires that make us attractive to one another, boys and girls, men and women. But with that urge must be self-discipline, rigid and strong and unbending."[2]

Many young people think they can hide their sins. "If no one knows," they say to themselves, "everything will be all right."

Sadly, that isn't true. President Spencer W. Kimball makes it plain that no one can hide anything from the Lord. Repentance is the only answer. He said, "All unchastity will one day be disclosed. There comes a time when the fornicator, like the murderer, wishes he could hide—hide from all the world, from all the ghosts, and especially his own, but there is no place to hide. There are dark corners and hidden spots and closed cars in which the transgression can be committed, but to totally conceal it is impossible.

"There is no night so dark, no room so tightly locked, no canyon so closed in, no desert so totally uninhabited that one can find a place to hide from his sins, from himself, or from the Lord. Eventually, one must face the great Maker."[3]

Sexual sins come in a great variety. To help you plainly understand what the Lord expects, these sins have been separated into categories.

Abortion

When a young woman is involved in sexual sin and finds herself pregnant, it can seem as if the whole world is crashing down on her. As a million thoughts go through her head, abortion might seem like an option. But this is what the Lord's prophets have said:

"Abortion is not the answer," President Gordon B. Hinckley said. "This only compounds the problem. It is an evil and repulsive escape that will someday bring regret and sorrow."[4]

President Spencer W. Kimball said, "Abortion, the taking of life, is one of the most grievous of sins. We have repeatedly affirmed the position of the Church in unalterably opposing all abortions, except in two rare instances: When conception is the result of forcible rape and when competent medical counsel indicates that a mother's health would otherwise be seriously jeopardized."[5]

The Church's current policy is that whenever possible, an expecting unwed mother who has no plans to marry should arrange to give the child up for adoption through LDS Family Services. If you are facing such a decision, talk with your bishop and parents. Studies have shown that this decision is best for both the mother and child, since the baby will be placed in a strong, two-parent LDS home.

LDS Family Services has a very good website at **www.itsaboutlove.org** that provides all the information you might need.

As President Kimball said, the only times abortion would even be considered would involve cases of rape or if the mother's life is in danger. Church leaders have also included incest (sexual relations between close relatives) as a possible reason for an abortion. Even then, the prophets caution, much thought should go into deciding whether to end the pregnancy.

Homosexuality

Every new television season seems to include a show that revolves around a homosexual theme or character. This is another case of the world accepting what Heavenly Father has forbidden.

Thousands of years ago, the cities of Sodom and Gomorrah were destroyed by the Lord because of this sin, and the Lord's policies haven't changed.

It is possible for a person to have homosexual tendencies, but that does not free him or her from living the law of chastity, just like someone who has heterosexual feelings. President Kimball said, "Homosexual conduct is serious sin. The unholy transgression of homosexuality is either rapidly growing, or tolerance is giving it wider publicity. If one has such desires and tendencies, he overcomes them the same as if he had the urge toward petting or fornication or adultery. The Lord condemns and forbids this practice with a vigor equal to his condemnation of adultery and other such sex acts. And the Church will excommunicate as readily any unrepentant addict.

"Again, contrary to the belief and statement of many people, this sin, like fornication, is overcomable and forgivable, but again, only upon a deep and abiding repentance, which means total abandonment and complete transformation of thought and act. The fact that some governments and some churches and numerous corrupted individuals have tried to reduce such behavior from criminal offense to personal privilege does not change the nature nor the seriousness of the practice. Good men, wise men, God-fearing men everywhere still denounce the practice as being unworthy of sons of God; and Christ's church denounces it and condemns it."[6]

Kissing

It is rare for people to break the law of chastity without first engaging in kissing. Don't give your kisses away like they are candy. Be wise in who you kiss—and don't feel obligated to kiss anyone.

Teenagers who suddenly find themselves buried in

sexual sin could have saved themselves so much heartache if they had been more cautious in guarding their kisses.

It is a matter of progression. It is hard to be swept down a raging river if you stay on dry land. But if you start wading out into the current—kiss by kiss—you might find it increasingly harder to get back to shore. And sadly, you might find yourself swept farther downstream than you ever could have imagined.

President Spencer W. Kimball said, "To kiss in casual dating is asking for trouble. What do kisses mean when given out like pretzels and robbed of sacredness? What is miscalled the 'soul kiss' (also known as the French kiss) is an abomination and stirs passions to the eventual loss of virtue. Even if timely courtship justifies the kiss it should be a clean, decent, sexless one."

President Kimball then says, "If the 'soul kiss' with its passion were eliminated from dating there would be an immediate upswing in chastity and honor, with fewer illegitimate babies, fewer unwed mothers, fewer forced marriages, and fewer unhappy people."[7]

Love versus lust

Too often young people confuse physical contact as being "love." Love is a matter of the heart and mind, not the body. President Hinckley said, "True love is not so much a matter of romance as it is a matter of anxious concern for the well-being of one's companion."[8]

President Ezra Taft Benson said it plainly, "Do not be misled by Satan's lies. There is no lasting happiness in immorality. There is no joy to be found in breaking the law of chastity. Just the opposite is true. There may be momentary pleasure. For a time it may seem like everything is wonderful. But quickly the relationship will sour. Guilt and shame set in. We become fearful that our sins will be discovered. We must sneak and hide, lie and cheat. Love begins to die. Bitterness, jealousy, anger, and even hate begin to grow. All of these are the natural results of sin and transgression.

"On the other hand, when we obey the law of chastity and keep ourselves morally clean, we will experience the blessings of increased love and peace, greater trust and respect for our marital partners, deeper commitment to each other, and, therefore, a deep and significant sense of joy and happiness."[9]

President Kimball gave these valuable insights: "If one really loves another, one would rather die for that person than to injure him. At the hour of sin, pure love is pushed out of one door while lust sneaks in the other. Affection has then been replaced with desire of the flesh and uncontrolled passion. Accepted has been the doctrine which the devil is so eager to establish, that illicit sex relations are justified. When the unmarried yield to lust, that is called fornication. When married fall into this same sin, that is called adultery.

"In order to live with themselves, people who transgress must follow one path or the other of two alternatives. The one is to sear the conscience or to dull the sensitivity with mental tranquilizers so that the transgressing may be continued. The other is to permit remorse to lead to total sorrow, repentance, and eventual forgiveness."[10]

Masturbation

This is a sin that Satan would love to have you rationalize, because it can open the door to much greater sins.

Webster's Dictionary defines it as "touching oneself for sexual gratification." This is another sin that the world and entertainment industry have tried to say is acceptable, but it is not acceptable to the Lord.

President Spencer W. Kimball said, "Prophets anciently and today condemn masturbation. It induces feelings of guilt and shame. It is detrimental to spirituality. It indicates slavery to the flesh, not that mastery of it and the growth toward godhood which is the object of our mortal life."[11]

President Kimball also said, "Masturbation, a rather common indiscretion, is not approved of the Lord nor of his church, regardless of what may have been said by others whose 'norms' are lower. Latter-day Saints are urged to avoid this practice. Anyone fettered by this weakness should abandon the habit before he goes on a mission or receives the holy priesthood or goes in the temple for his blessings."[12]

Necking and petting

Growing up, I heard many church leaders condemn "necking and petting." But there was one problem—they never really defined it! As a deacon, I had no idea what they were talking about, and many of my friends felt the same way. When it came to "necking" we imagined some strange ritual where a boy and girl somehow wrapped their necks around each other.

I had seen some relay games at our ward youth activity where we would hold an egg under our chins and then attempt to pass it to someone else without using our hands. It surprised me that such a game would be played at a church activity, because that game came awful close to what I thought necking was—and I still couldn't see how that would bring much pleasure.

"Petting" was another activity I was very cautious about—I made sure I never patted the head or hair of any girl. Maybe you have felt the same confusion.

On a more serious note, those two terms are gentle ways to describe some all-too-common sins. Necking is also known as "making out." Like most sexual sins, there are certainly different levels of this transgression, but once open-mouth or French kissing becomes part of the routine, you are in dangerous territory. President Kimball helps clarify it. He said, "With the absence of the 'soul kiss,' necking would be greatly reduced. The younger sister of petting, it should be totally eliminated. Both are abominations in their own right."[13]

As President Kimball said, necking is the younger sibling of petting. Petting is when "making out" goes well beyond proper boundaries. It involves the touching and fondling of private, sacred parts of each other's bodies, either through clothing or in direct contact.

President Kimball once again explains what the Lord's stand is on the issue. He said, "Among the most common sexual sins our young people commit are necking and petting. Not only do these improper relations often lead to fornication, pregnancy, and abortions—all ugly sins—but in and of themselves they are pernicious evils, and it is often difficult for youth to distinguish where one ends and another begins. They awaken lust and stir evil thoughts and sex desires.

"They are but parts of the whole family of related sins and indiscretions. Paul (the apostle) wrote as if to modern young people who deceive themselves that their necking and petting are but expressions of love: 'Wherefore God also gave them up to uncleanness through the lusts of their own hearts, to dishonour their own bodies between themselves.' How could the evils of petting be more completely described?"

President Kimball added, "Our young people should know that their partners in sin will not love or respect them if they have freedom in fondling their bodies. Such a practice destroys respect, not only for the other person but for self. It destroys the ultimate respect for virtue.

"Too many have lost themselves completely in sin through this doorway of necking and petting. The devil knows how to destroy our young girls and boys. He may not be able to tempt a person to murder or to commit adultery immediately, but he knows that if he can get a boy and a girl to sit in the car late enough after the dance, or to park long enough in the dark at the end of the lane, the best boy and the best girl will finally succumb and fall. He knows that all have a limit to their resistance."[14]

If you are involved in such activities, decide to stop immediately. It might be one of the most painful decisions you make, but you will be grateful you did. If your partner urges you to continue such acts, you have received your answer concerning whether your relationship is based on "love" or "lust." As you put the sin of petting in your past, discuss with your bishop the process of repentance. He can help you begin the path to full forgiveness.

Sexual relations within marriage are good and honorable. They bind couples together in love. But such activities outside of marriage can lead to spiritual disaster. Engaged couples preparing for temple marriage must keep their standards high as the wedding date grows closer. Nothing is more heartbreaking than the postponement of a temple marriage due to unworthiness.

President Joseph F. Smith said, "Sexual union is lawful in wedlock, and if participated in with right intent is honorable and sanctifying. But without the bonds of marriage, sexual indulgence is a debasing sin, abominable in the sight of Deity. . . We hold that sexual sin is second only to the shedding of innocent blood in the category of personal crimes."[15]

Pornography

Pornography is defined by Webster's Dictionary as "writings and pictures intended to arouse sexual desire." Such material was once tucked away and not readily available to the general public. Laws were designed to keep it from being sold openly. But with the invention of the Internet, pornography has spread across the world. At the same time, magazines that would never have been allowed on store newsstands are now openly displayed.

Sadly, it seems no law or government can halt it. So now it is up to each individual to avoid it at all costs.

Concerning pornography, President Gordon B. Hinckley said, "Leave it alone! Get away from it! Avoid it! It is sleazy filth! It is rot that will do no good! You cannot afford to watch videotapes of this kind of stuff. You cannot afford to read magazines that are designed to destroy you. You can't do it, nor even watch it on television. Stay away from it! Avoid it like the plague because it is just as deadly, more so. The plague will destroy the body. Pornography will destroy the body and the soul. Stay away from it! It is as a great disease that is sweeping over the country and over the entire world. Avoid it! I repeat, avoid it!"[16]

At a BYU devotional, President Hinckley gave these comments. "Pornography is the literature of the devil," he said. "Shun it. Stay away from it. Lift your sights and your minds to the higher and nobler things of life. Remember, 'wickedness never was happiness.' (Alma 41:10) Sin never brought happiness. Transgression never brought happiness. Disobedience never brought happiness.

"Recognize pornography for what it is—a vicious brew of slime and sleaze, the partaking of which only leads to misery, degradation, and regret. The Church expects you who have taken upon yourselves the name of the Lord Jesus Christ to walk in the sunlight of virtue and enjoy the strength, the freedom, the lift that come from so doing."[17]

President Kimball made it clear that Church members are expected to consciously avoid such material. He said, "Each person must keep himself clean and free from lusts. He must shun ugly, polluted thoughts and acts as he would an enemy.

"Pornography and erotic stories and pictures are worse than polluted food. Shun them. The body has power to rid itself of sickening food. That person who entertains filthy stories or pornographic pictures and literature records them in his marvelous human computer, the brain, which can't forget this filth. Once recorded, it will always remain there, subject to recall filthy images."[18]

Words to live by:

Ezra Taft Benson: In the Church and kingdom of God, chastity will never be out of date, regardless of what the world may do or say. So we say to you, young men and women—maintain your self-respect. Do not engage in intimacies that bring heartache and sorrow. You cannot build happy lives on immorality.[19]

Spencer W. Kimball: When the sun grows cold and the stars no longer shine, the law of chastity will still be basic in God's world and in the Lord's church. Old values are upheld by the Church not because they are old, but rather because through the ages they have proved right. It will always be the rule.[20]

Joseph F. Smith: We desire with holy zeal to emphasize the enormity of sexual sins. Though often regarded as insignificant by those not knowing the will of God, they are in his eyes an abomination, and if we are to remain his favored people they must be shunned as the gates of hell.

The evil results of these sins are so patent in vice, crime, misery and disease that it would appear that all, young and old, must perceive and sense them. They are destroying the world.

If we are to be preserved we must abhor them, shun them, not practice the least of them—for they weaken and kill man spiritually. They make him unfit for the company of the righteous and the presence of God.[21]

CHAPTER 28

SUNDAY ACTIVITIES

And he commanded them that they
should observe the Sabbath day,
and keep it holy, and also every day
they should give thanks to the Lord their God.
Mosiah 18:23

On the morning of Tuesday, Sept. 11, 2001, I got up and turned on the TV. All the news programs were showing the Twin Towers of New York City's World Trade Center. One of the towers had smoke pouring out of it. I had served a mission in New Jersey and had looked across the Hudson River at those towers almost every day for two years, so it bothered me to see such a sight.

The news commentators were saying an airplane had accidentally hit the tower. But at that moment another plane darted across the screen and hit the other tower. Thus began possibly the worst day most Americans have ever experienced.

The following Sunday our Sacrament Meeting was overflowing. We had to set up folding chairs in the cultural hall. We saw many faces we hadn't seen at church in a long time. Three of our finest speakers in the ward gave inspiring, patriotic messages, and every prayer included a heartfelt plea for Heavenly Father's protection and guidance. The future was uncertain, and suddenly everyone was energized to live righteously.

The following Sunday the chapel was full again, but as the weeks went by and the terrorists were on the run, church attendance dwindled again to normal numbers.

Here's the question: Does the Lord value our church attendance more when there is a great crisis, or when life is relatively calm?

Here is President Spencer W. Kimball's description of typical Sabbath days he had witnessed. "While attending one of the conferences last fall, I was housed in a hotel, and early Sunday morning I was awakened by considerable noise in the halls and the lobby of the hotel. When I came down I found that the lobby and the café near it were filled with men with colored shirts and caps and with hunting regalia. Their guns were clean and shining. They were all en route to the mountains and the canyons to get their deer. When the conference day was ended and evening found us on our way home, many were the cars that we passed with a deer on the running board or on the bumper.

"Another Sabbath I drove through an agricultural area, and was distressed to find there were mowing machines and balers and perspiring men engaged in harvesting the crops.

"Still another Sabbath I drove through Main Street of one of our larger towns, and I was dismayed to find lines of people standing and waiting their turns to get into the picture shows.

"Still another time when large numbers of people with hiking breeches and slacks were driving to mountain retreats with picnic lunches to enjoy the beauteous Sabbath in the canyons.

"And the word of the Lord continued to resound in my consciousness: 'In the days of their peace they esteemed lightly of my counsel; but in the day of their trouble, of necessity they feel after me.' I wondered if we must be brought low with adversity before we will serve the Lord."

President Kimball continued, "There came ringing again in my ears the solemn command brought down from the thundering of Mount Sinai: 'Remember the sabbath day, to keep it holy.' So far as I know, that commandment has never been rescinded nor modified. To hunt and fish on the Lord's day is not keeping it holy. To plant or cultivate or harvest crops on the Sabbath is not keeping holy the Lord's day. To go into the canyons for picnics, to attend games or rodeos, or races, or shows, or other amusements on that day is not to keep it in holy remembrance. . .

"The Church favors legitimate recreation, and urges its people to organize picnic parties and to enjoy the great outdoors for the fellowship that it offers, but with six other days in the week, the Sabbath certainly need not be desecrated. I think it isn't so much a matter of giving up things; it is a matter of shifting times and choosing seasons."[1]

Let's look at other aspects of the Sabbath day.

Attendance at Sunday meetings

Attending our Sunday meetings is not only a commandment (see D&C 20:75 and also D&C 59:9), but it is the key to keeping the Spirit with us. President Gordon B. Hinckley said, "I feel in my heart that if every member of the Church would resolve within himself or herself that they would partake of the sacrament every week, if possible, we would have greater spirituality and we would have fewer defaults, as it were, among our membership."[2]

President Kimball faced the issue of Church members disregarding the Sabbath day throughout his apostleship.

He told of one friend in particular that caused him great concern. His friend remained home each Sabbath and justified himself by saying that he could benefit more by reading a good book at home than by attending the sacrament meeting and listening to a poor sermon.

This was President Kimball's response. He told the man, "The home, sacred as it should be, is not the house of prayer. In it no sacrament is administered; in it is not found the fellowship with members, nor the confession of sins to the brethren. The mountains may be termed the temples of God and the forests and streams his handiwork, but only in the meetinghouse, or house of prayer, can be fulfilled all the requirements of the Lord."[3]

The sacrament is the crowning moment of Sunday meetings. President John Taylor said, "In partaking of the sacrament we not only commemorate the death and sufferings of our Lord and Savior Jesus Christ, but we also shadow forth the time when he will come again and when we shall meet and eat bread with him in the kingdom of God. When we are thus assembled together, we may expect to receive guidance and blessings from God."[4]

Outdoor recreation on Sunday

Many of the prophets have spoken out on letting Sunday become a "recreation day." George Albert Smith said, "The Sabbath has become the play-day of this great nation—the day set apart by thousands to violate the commandment that God gave long, long ago, and I am persuaded that much of the sorrow and distress that is afflicting and will continue to inflict mankind is traceable to the fact that they have ignored his admonition to keep the Sabbath day holy."[5]

President Heber J. Grant give similar counsel. He said, "A sacred Sabbath is not going out on excursions on Sunday. A sacred Sabbath is to attend our meetings and to read the Scriptures, to supplicate God, and to have our minds set upon the things that are calculated to save us in this life and in the life to come."[6]

Productive Sunday activities

Sometimes it might feel like the prophets are saying you can't do *anything* on Sunday except go to Church. However, the opposite is true.

They encourage members to do many activities that tend to get overlooked the rest of the week. President Kimball gave a list of activities that families or individuals could consider doing on the Sabbath day. He mentioned we could:

* Read the scriptures and Church publications
* Study the lives and teachings of the prophets
* Prepare Church lessons for the following week
* Write in a journal or work on a personal history
* Visit relatives and friends
* Write to missionaries
* Enjoy uplifting music and sing Church hymns
* Hold family council meetings
* Discuss gospel topics
* Read with a child
* Do family history research
* Read uplifting literature
* Plan the upcoming Family Night lesson
* Build friendships with neighbors
* Visit the sick, the aged, and the lonely
* And finally, pray and meditate [7]

What about doing homework on Sunday? President Kimball gave this counsel: "Studying on the Sabbath should be minimal. I hope students will use the Sabbath for studying only as an emergency. I believe that generally, with careful organization of time through the week, most studying can be done on weekdays, leaving the Sabbath for worship."

He added, "There might be times when one would feel forced to study, when he might feel that it was an ox in the mire. I am expressing only my personal opinions on this matter, but since we are talking to students, it would be my hope that your studying could be done in the season thereof and not as a cramming process just before you go on Monday mornings."[8]

Shopping on Sunday

Few topics seem to be ignored more consistently by the members of the Church than this one. It must be frustrating to the General Authorities as they travel throughout Utah on Sunday and see as many cars in the grocery store parking lot as there are at the church.

President Gordon B. Hinckley said, "It appalls me to see Latter-day Saints who shop on Sunday. I cannot understand how they can go in the face of the direct word of the Lord that 'thou shalt keep the Sabbath day holy.' Shopping is not a part of keeping the Sabbath day holy."[9]

President Hinckley has also said, "It is a sad thing to me to see stores open on the Sabbath Day. But we do not need to shop on the Sabbath. Nobody needs to shop on the Sabbath. You can buy enough meat on Saturday to get through Sunday. You can buy enough milk on Saturday to get through Sunday. The bread will not get unduly stale when it is bought on Saturday to be used on Sunday. You certainly do not need to buy clothing on Sunday nor furniture nor anything of that kind. Keep the Sabbath day holy."[10]

President Kimball said, "Sabbath-breakers are those who buy commodities or entertainment on the Sabbath, thus encouraging pleasure palaces and business establishments to remain open—which they otherwise would not do."[11]

Working on Sunday

It is a fact of our modern world that some people must work on the Sabbath. And, in fact, some of the work that is truly necessary—such as caring for the sick—serves to honor the Sabbath. However, in such activities our motives are a most important consideration.

President Kimball said, "Many good folk are compelled to labor on Sunday. Their alternatives are to work or lose their employment. But frequently those whose shift work occupies part of the day excuse themselves from Sabbath activities, using their work as an alibi. Shift workers seldom work more hours a day than other folk, and if they are determined, such people can usually find ample time to render service and to hallow the Sabbath in the hours that remain.

"Can the employer rest easy in his pew at church while his employees make profits for his bank account on the Sabbath? Can the parents fully enjoy their meetings having hired baby-sitters to watch their children, who also should attend Sabbath meetings?"[12]

The decision to work on Sunday is ultimately between you and the Lord.

Words to Live By:

Gordon B. Hinckley: Let us not let down our standards. Keep the boats at home on Sunday.[13]

Spencer W. Kimball: Strange as it may seem, some Latter-day Saints, faithful in all other respects, justify themselves in missing their church meetings on occasion for recreational purposes, feeling that the best fishing will be missed if one is not on the stream on opening day or that the vacation will not be long enough if one does not set off on Sunday or that one will miss a movie he wanted to see if he does not go on the Sabbath. And in their breach of the Sabbath they often take their families with them.[14]

Harold B. Lee: It's all right to pull the cow out of the mud on Sunday, provided that you don't push him in on Saturday night.[15]

Joseph F. Smith: To observe the Sabbath day properly is the plain duty of every Latter-day Saint—and that includes the young men and young women and the boys and girls. It may seem strange that it should be necessary to repeat this often-asserted fact. But there appear to be some people, and sometimes whole communities, who neglect this duty, and therefore stand in need of this admonition.

What are we required to do on the Sabbath day? The revelations of the Lord to the Prophet Joseph are very plain on this subject, and these should govern us, for they are in strict harmony with the teachings of the Savior. Here are some of the simple requirements:

The Sabbath is appointed unto you to rest from your

labors. Men are not resting from their labors when they plow, and plant and haul and dig. They are not resting when they linger around the home all day on Sunday, doing odd jobs that they have been too busy to do on other days.

Men are not showing zeal and ardor in their religious faith and duty when they hustle off early Sunday morning in automobiles to the canyons, the resorts, and to places of amusement with their wives and children. They are not paying their devotions in this way to the Most High.

In seeking pleasure and recreation, they do not offer their time and attention in the worship of the Lord; nor can they thus rejoice in the spirit of forgiveness and worship that comes with partaking of the holy sacrament.

Boys and young men are not fasting with singleness of heart that their joy may be full when they spend the Sabbath day loafing around the ice-cream stand or restaurant, playing games, or in riding, fishing, shooting, or engaged in physical sports, excursions and outings.

Such is not the course that will keep them unspotted from the world, but rather one that will deprive them of the rich promises of the Lord, giving them sorrow instead of joy, and unrest and anxiety instead of the peace that comes with works of righteousness.

Let us play and take recreation to our hearts' content during other days, but on the Sabbath let us rest, worship, go to the house of prayer, partake of the sacrament, eat our food with singleness of heart, and pay our devotions to God, that the fulness of the earth may be ours, and that we may have peace in this world and eternal life in the world to come.

"But," says one, "in our settlement we have no other day for amusement and sports, excursions and outings, ball games and races."

Then demand one.

Is it possible that parents—in the face of the promises of the Lord—will force their children to spend the Sabbath in sports?[16]

CHAPTER 29

SWEARING

Behold, I am Alpha and Omega, even Jesus Christ. Wherefore, let all men beware how they take my name in their lips—For behold, verily I say, that many there be who are under this condemnation, who use the name of the Lord, and use it in vain, having not authority.
D&C 63:61-62

A sad reflection on our society is the casual use of the Lord's name in vain—and other swear words—in television shows and music, usually in an effort to make people laugh. It is not a laughing matter to the Lord, though.

The word "God" is used properly in prayers, and in the scriptures. But much more often the phrase is heard as an angry, sarcastic or surprised exclamation. It seems the vocabulary of some people is so limited that they can't hardly say anything else. The same goes with the common four-letter words that are heard all throughout society.

Contrast the profanity we hear all around us to this story from the life of President Spencer W. Kimball. He was in the hospital one day for an operation, and was being wheeled out of the operating room. The attendant stumbled, and from the man's mouth came vicious cursing, including a combination of the names of the Savior.

President Kimball was only half-conscious, but he

recoiled and said to the attendant, "Please! Please! That is my Lord whose names you revile." There was a deathly silence, then the attendant whispered, "I am sorry."[1]

President Gordon B. Hinckley has said, "Stay out of the gutter in your conversation. Foul talk defiles the man who speaks it. . . . Don't swear. Don't profane. Avoid so-called dirty jokes. Stay away from conversation that is sprinkled with foul and filthy words. You will be happier if you do so, and your example will give strength to others."[2]

As a teenager I worked as a member of a parks maintenance crew, and each morning we would meet at our main office, then pile into a truck to travel to whatever project we were working on that day.

The person who would drive us to each project was a middle-aged man who was the nicest guy in the world— but he couldn't resist telling us teenage boys some off-color jokes.

It was uncomfortable for me, but I stayed silent. Day after day that summer, this man would tell us these dirty jokes. As the summer went on, the jokes kept getting worse. Finally a fellow employee told the man, "Knock it off! We've heard enough."

It worked—the man stopped telling the jokes. I only wish I had showed that same type of courage earlier in the summer, because twenty years later some of those crude, dirty jokes still roll into my mind once in a while.

You have likely heard that your mind is like a computer. It records everything you see and hear, so if something is going on around you that you don't like, put a stop to it. Don't be silent like I was.

Along those lines, President Joseph F. Smith said, "There is something in man, an essential part of his mind, which recalls the events of the past, and the words that we have spoken on various occasions. Words which we spoke in our childhood we can readily bring to mind. Words that we heard others speak in our infancy, we can recall, though we may be advanced in years. We recall words that were spoken in our youth and in our early manhood, as well as words that were spoken yesterday.

"May I say to you that in reality a man cannot forget anything? He may have a lapse of memory; he may not be able to recall at the moment a thing that he knows, or words that he has spoken; he may not have the power at his will to call up these events and words; but let God Almighty touch the mainspring of the memory, and awaken recollection, and you will find then that you have not even forgotten a single idle word that you have spoken.

"I believe the word of God to be true, and therefore, I warn the youth of Zion, as well as those who are advanced in years, to beware of saying wicked things, of speaking evil, and taking in vain the name of sacred things and sacred beings. Guard your words, that you may not offend even man, much less offend God."[3]

Words to live by:

Joseph Fielding Smith: Profanity is filthiness. A person is known as much by his language as he is by the company he keeps.[4]

David O. McKay: Swearing is a vice that bespeaks a low standard of breeding. Blasphemous exclamations drive out all spirit of reverence.[5]

CHAPTER 30

TEMPLE COVENANTS

And again, verily I say unto you, if a man marry a
wife by my word, which is my law,
and by the new and everlasting covenant,
and it is sealed unto them by the Holy Spirit of
promise, by him who is appointed, unto whom
I have appointed this power and the keys
of this priesthood; and it shall be said unto them—
Ye shall come forth in the first resurrection. . .
and shall inherit thrones, kingdoms, principalities,
and powers . . . and they shall pass by the angels,
and the gods, which are set there,
to their exaltation and glory in all things,
as hath been sealed upon their heads.
D&C 132:19

There is the old saying, "You can't take it with you when you die." That applies to nearly everything—but not temple covenants. Read again the scripture at the top of this page.

The scripture makes it plain that if we follow the Lord's commandments, and make holy covenants in the temple, we can take our family with us beyond the grave and into the eternities.

The world does not comprehend the power that is contained within the ordinances of the temple. In effect, in the temple we promise the Lord we will do all we can to keep his commandments and serve others, and in return the Lord promises to give us all that he has. Nothing should be more important to us in this life than being worthy to enter the temple—and then doing so.

The importance of the temple ordinances was made plain when the spirits of some of the most prominent men in world history requested that their temple work be done.

It happened in 1877 when President Wilford Woodruff was serving as the president of the St. George Temple. Speaking of that experience, President Woodruff said:

"The spirits of the dead gathered around me, wanting to know why we did not redeem them. Said they, 'You have had the use of the Endowment House for a number of years, and yet nothing has ever been done for us. We laid the foundation of the government you now enjoy, and we never apostatized from it, but we remained true to it and were faithful to God.' These were the signers of the Declaration of Independence, and they waited on me for two days and two nights. I thought it very singular, that notwithstanding so much work had been done, and yet nothing had been done for them.

"The thought never entered my heart, from the fact, I suppose, that heretofore our minds were reaching after our more immediate friends and relatives. I straightway went into the baptismal font [in the temple] and called upon brother McCallister to baptize me for the signers of the Declaration of Independence, and fifty other eminent men, making one hundred in all, including John Wesley, Columbus, and others."[1]

President Gordon B. Hinckley said, "Until you have received the sacred [temple] ordinances of the gospel, you have not received all of the wonderful blessings which this Church has to offer. The great and crowning blessings of membership in The Church of Jesus Christ of Latter-day Saints are those blessings which come to us in the house of the Lord."[2]

President Harold B. Lee explained, "When you enter a holy temple, you are by that course gaining fellowship with the saints in God's eternal kingdom, where time is no more. In the temples of your God you are endowed not with a rich legacy of worldly treasure, but with a wealth of eternal riches that are above price.

"The temple ceremonies are designed by a wise Heavenly Father who has revealed them to us in these last days as a guide and a protection throughout our lives, that you and I might not fail to merit exaltation in the celestial kingdom where God and Christ dwell."[3]

Celestial marriage

The crowning ordinance of the temple is the sealing of a man and a woman together for eternity—commonly referred to as a temple marriage or celestial marriage.

President Ezra Taft Benson said, "Understand that temple marriage is essential to your salvation and exaltation. . . . Honorable marriage is more important than wealth, position, and status. As husband and wife, you can achieve your life's goals together. As you sacrifice for each other and your children, the Lord will bless you, and your commitment to the Lord and your service in His kingdom will be enhanced."[4]

Joseph F. Smith explained the order of heaven—exaltation in the highest degree of the celestial kingdom comes only to those who are sealed as couples in the temple. He said, "The woman will not go there alone, and the man will not go there alone, and claim exaltation. They may attain a degree of salvation alone, but when they are exalted they will be exalted according to the law of the celestial kingdom. They cannot be exalted in any other way, neither the living nor the dead."[5]

For that reason alone, temple marriage should be one of your highest priorities in life. Don't settle for less.

Family history work

A vast number of missionaries are currently at work, part of a large, organized network that is reaching people who have never heard the gospel.

But they aren't serving here in the mortal world—this particular army of missionaries works in the Spirit World.

Joseph F. Smith said, "This gospel revealed to the Prophet Joseph is already being preached to the spirits in prison, to those who have passed away from this stage of action into the spirit world without the knowledge of the gospel. Joseph Smith is preaching that gospel to them. So is Hyrum Smith. So is Brigham Young, and so are all the faithful apostles that lived in this dispensation under the administration of the Prophet Joseph.

"They are there, having carried with them from here the holy Priesthood that they received under authority, and which was conferred upon them in the flesh; they are preaching the gospel to the spirits in prison; for Christ, when his body lay in the tomb, went to proclaim liberty to the captives and opened the prison doors to them that were bound.

"Not only are these engaged in that work but hundreds and thousands of others; the elders that have died in the mission field have not finished their missions, but they are continuing them in the spirit world."[6]

That is the purpose of temple work—to do the ordinance work for these people who died without hearing the gospel, but who have now accepted it in the Spirit World.

President Wilford Woodruff said, "We have a great work before us in the redemption of our dead. Those persons may receive their testimony, but they cannot be baptized in the spirit world, for somebody on the earth must perform this ordinance for them in the flesh before they can receive part in the first resurrection and be worthy of eternal life.

"It takes as much to save a dead man as a living one. Have we any time to spend in trying to get rich and in neglecting our dead? I tell you no."[7]

Temple work not only blesses those in the Spirit World, but also those of us who attend the temple. It is a form of service that also lifts our spirits and brings greater spirituality into our lives.

President Gordon B. Hinckley said, "I hope that everyone gets to the temple on a regular basis. I hope your children over twelve years of age have the opportunity of going to the temple to be baptized for the dead. If we are a temple-going people, we will be a better people.

"I know your lives are busy. I know that you have much to do. But I make you a promise that if you will go to the house of the Lord, you will be blessed, and life will be better for you."[8]

Words to live by:

Heber J. Grant: I believe that no worthy young Latter-day Saint man or woman should spare any reasonable effort to come to a house of the Lord to begin life together. The marriage vows taken in these hallowed places and the sacred covenants entered into for time and all eternity are proof against many of the temptations of life that tend to break homes and destroy happiness.[9]

Lorenzo Snow: When we go back into the other life and find our dead friends living there, if we have not performed the labor that is necessary for their exaltation and glory we shall not feel very happy and it will not be a very pleasant meeting.[10]

Brigham Young: Your endowment is to receive all those ordinances in the House of the Lord, which are necessary for you, after you have departed this life, to enable you to walk back to the presence of the Father, passing the angels who stand as sentinels, being enabled to give them the key words, the signs and tokens, pertaining to the holy priesthood, and gain your eternal exaltation.[11]

Joseph Smith: The greatest responsibility in this world that God has laid upon us is to seek after our dead. Those Saints who neglect it, do it at the peril of their own salvation.[12]

CHAPTER 31

TEMPTATION

*"... humble yourselves before the Lord, and call on his
holy name, and watch and pray continually, that ye
may not be tempted above that which ye can bear,
and thus be led by the Holy Spirit,
becoming humble, meek, submissive, patient,
full of love, and all long-suffering."*
Alma 13:29

A key reason we are on earth is to be tested—to see how we respond to trials and opposition. As we reject temptation, we grow spiritually, and become more like our Heavenly Father.

Even the greatest people who have ever lived have faced temptation. Jesus was tempted by Satan, and Joseph Smith said that as a teenager, "I was left to all kinds of temptations; and, mingling with all kinds of society, I frequently fell into many foolish errors, and displayed the weakness of youth."[1]

So if you are struggling with temptation, you are not alone! With the Lord's help, you can overcome these trials.

The Lord told the prophet Moroni, "I give unto men weakness that they may be humble . . . and if they humble themselves before me, and have faith in me, then will I make weak things become strong unto them." (Ether 12:27)

If we succumb to temptation, we are accountable for our actions. We can't shift the blame to someone else. President Gordon B. Hinckley has said, "You have a responsibility to keep your minds clean from bad and evil thoughts—from anything which would lower your thoughts into that which is filthy, instead of that which is beautiful and bright and wholesome."[2]

President Spencer W. Kimball hoped every boy and girl would promise themselves, "I will not yield," before they were faced with temptation. Then when they were tempted in some way, they could say, "No, I won't sin. I have already made up my mind. That's settled."[3]

In many ways, the *Star Wars* movies parallel real life. There are opposing powers constantly at work. *Star Wars* creator George Lucas refers to them as "The Force" and "The Dark Side." We know them simply as good and evil.

President George Albert Smith said, "There are two influences ever present in the world. One is constructive and elevating and comes from our Heavenly Father; the other is destructive and debasing and comes from Lucifer. We have our agency and make our own choices in life subject to these unseen powers.

"There is a division line well defined that separates the Lord's territory from Lucifer's. If we live on the Lord's side of the line, Lucifer cannot come there to influence us, but if we cross the line into his territory, we are in his power.

"By keeping the commandments of the Lord we are safe on His side of the line, but if we disobey His teachings we voluntarily cross into the zone of temptation and invite the destruction that is ever present there. Knowing this, how anxious we should always be to live on the Lord's side of the line."[4]

Clean thoughts

The power to overcome temptation begins in our minds. What we allow into our minds will determine what we become. President Ezra Taft Benson said, "Thoughts lead to acts, acts lead to habits, habits lead to character—and our character will determine our eternal destiny."[5]

President Spencer W. Kimball made a good point. He said, "How could a person possibly become what he is *not* thinking? Nor is any thought, when persistently entertained, too small to have its effect."[6]

President George Albert Smith said, "You will be held accountable for your thoughts, because when your life is completed in mortality, it will be the sum of your thoughts. That one suggestion had been a great blessing to me all my life, and it has enabled me upon many occasions to avoid thinking improperly, because I realize that I will be, when my life's labor is complete, the product of my thoughts."[7]

False doctrine

Sometimes rumors are spread by Church members—or teachings are given—that just don't feel right. But they seem to make sense. How can we determine if such things are true? Thankfully, there are ways we can recognize false doctrine. They include:

1. What do the standard works have to say about it?
2. What do the latter-day presidents of the Church say on the subject—particularly the living prophet?
3. The Holy Ghost—the test of the Spirit. By the Spirit we "may know the truth of all things."

When any teaching or doctrine is in conflict with or contrary to one or all of these requirements, it must be set aside as false.

When the Lord has something to reveal to the members of the Church, it will be through his prophet. Every few years, rumors seem to spread about messengers appearing and telling people about the future.

President Harold B. Lee responded to such rumors by saying, "When there is to be anything different from that which the Lord has told us already, he will give it to his prophet, not to some Tom, Dick or Harry that is thumbing his way across the country as we have had people tell the story; and not through someone, as another story relates, who swooned and came up and gave a revelation.

"I have said, 'Do you suppose that when the Lord has his prophet on the earth, that he is going to take some round-about means of revealing things to his children? That is what he has a prophet for, and when he has something to give to this Church, he will give it to the President, and the President will see that the presidents of stakes and missions get it, along with General Authorities; and they in turn will see that the people are advised of any new change.'

"A man came in to see me and said that he had heard that some man appeared mysteriously to a group of temple workers and told them, 'You had better hurry up and store food for a year or two, or three, because there will come a season when there won't be any production.' He asked me what I thought about it, and I said, 'Well, were you in the April Conference of 1936?'

"He replied, 'No, I couldn't be there.' And I said, 'Well, you surely read the report of what was said by the Brethren in that Conference?' No, he hadn't.

"'Well,' I said, 'at that Conference the Lord *did* give a revelation about the storage of food. How in the world is the Lord going to get over to you what he wants you to do if you are not there when he says it, and you do not take the time to read it after it has been said?'

"The Lord is going to keep his people informed, if they will listen. As President Clark said in a classic talk that he gave, 'What we need today is not more prophets. We have the prophets. But what we need is more people with listening ears. That is the great need of our generation.'"[8]

President Joseph F. Smith explained where most of the false doctrine within the church originates. He said, "Among the Latter-day Saints, the preaching of false doctrine disguised as truths of the gospel, may be expected from people of two classes, and practically from these only. They are:

"First—The hopelessly ignorant, whose lack of intelligence is due to their indolence and sloth, who make but feeble effort, if indeed any at all, to better themselves by reading and study; those who are afflicted with a dread disease that may soon develop into an incurable malady—laziness.

"Second—The proud and self-vaunting ones, who read by the lamp of their own conceit; who interpret by rules of their own contriving; who have become a law unto themselves, and so pose as the sole judges of their own doings. These are more dangerously ignorant than the first.

"Beware of the lazy and the proud; their infection in each case is contagious; better for them and for all when they are compelled to display the yellow flag of warning, that the clean and uninfected may be protected."[9]

Words to live by:

Howard W. Hunter: Jesus was not spared grief and pain and anguish and buffeting. No tongue can speak the unutterable burden he carried. Peace was on the lips and in the heart of the Savior no matter how fiercely the tempest was raging. May it so be with us—in our own hearts, in our own homes, in our nations of the world, and even in the buffeting faced from time to time by the Church. We should not expect to get through life individually and collectively without some opposition.[10]

Ezra Taft Benson: God loves us; the devil hates us. God wants us to have a fullness of joy as He has. The devil wants us to be miserable as he is. God gives us commandments to bless us. The devil would have us break these commandments to curse us.[11]

Spencer W. Kimball: Where there are challenges, you fail only if you fail to keep trying![12]

Joseph F. Smith: Among the strong helps to gain self-respect are personal purity and proper thoughts, which are the bases of all proper action. I wish that all young men could appreciate the value there is in this practice, and in giving their youthful days to the service of the Lord. Growth, development, progress, self-respect, the esteem and admiration of men naturally follow such a course in youth. The Savior set a striking example in this matter, and was early about his Father's business. He did not leave it until his older years, but even as early as twelve he had developed so far in this line that he was able to teach men of wisdom and doctors of knowledge in the temple.[13]

Lorenzo Snow: As soon as we discover ourselves in a fault, we should repent of the wrong-doing and as far as possible repair or make good the wrong we may have committed. By taking this course we strengthen our character, we advance our own cause, and we fortify ourselves against temptation.[14]

Brigham Young: If you first gain power to check your words you will then begin to have power to check your judgment, and at length actually gain power to check your thoughts and reflections.[15]

CHAPTER 32

TESTIMONY

"The scriptures are laid before thee, yea, and all things denote there is a God; yea, even the earth, and all things that are upon the face of it, yea, and its motion, yea, and also all the planets which move in their regular form do witness that there is a Supreme Creator.
Alma 30: 44

The apostate Nephite named Korihor once challenged Alma to give him a sign that God exists. Alma had been debating with Korihor for quite a while, and finally Alma explained in the above scripture that everything in and above the earth is a testimony of God, even the orbits of the planets.

Of course, this makes sense to those who have a testimony, but what if you aren't sure you even have one yet?

If you are having doubts, a good place to start is with Alma's words. He mentions how even the planets themselves testify of God. Look at the sky at night, and ponder the great order in the universe—the planets, the stars.

The first time I really pondered the universe and all of God's creations, I went for a walk around the block at about 9 p.m. I looked up at the sky and clearly saw the constellation known as The Big Dipper.

I stared at it, and realized that each point of the Big Dipper is a star, created by our Heavenly Father. For some reason, it helped me find my place in life—a child of God. I realized there were greater things in the universe than the trials I then faced, such as making the high school baseball team or surviving trigonometry. Those things were important, but not the *most* important things in life.

Even now, when life gets a little hectic, I walk out into the night and look at The Big Dipper, and everything comes back into perspective—that God lives; that we are His children; that this life is just a test, and if we pass the test, we will live again with Heavenly Father.

Of course, gaining a testimony takes effort on our part. A testimony is a living thing. In Alma chapter 32, in the Book of Mormon, Alma compares a new testimony to a seed. This seed must be fed and cared for. Then it will begin to take root. As it grows, Alma says, "it shall be a tree springing up unto everlasting life." (Alma 32:41)

Picture your testimony as a newly planted tree. It won't stay in the same condition for very long. It will either grow and produce fruit, or it will wilt and die. Your efforts will determine whether it grows into a strong "tree" or wastes away from lack of nourishment. It is a process we each must go through.

President Howard W. Hunter said, "I have sympathy for young men and young women when honest doubts enter their minds and they engage in the great conflict of resolving doubts. These doubts can be resolved, if they have an honest desire to know the truth, by exercising moral, spiritual, and mental effort.

"They will emerge from the conflict into a firmer, stronger, larger faith because of the struggle. They have gone from a simple, trusting faith, through doubt and conflict, into a solid substantial faith which ripens into testimony."[1]

It is possible to develop a strong testimony at a young age. Such was the case with President Joseph F. Smith when he returned home from his mission to Hawaii in 1857. He came home through California, and in those days most people in the United States didn't really understand Mormonism. The nation's newspapers would print false statements about the Church, so there was much excitement and bitter feelings concerning the Mormons.

Joseph's wagon train had just made their camp one evening outside of Los Angeles when several rough-looking men rode up on horseback. These men were threatening to hurt or even kill any Mormons they saw.

When the men arrived, Joseph was away from the camp gathering wood for the fire. He returned to see that the members of his camp had cautiously gone into the brush down the creek, out of sight. When he saw that, he thought, "Shall I run from these fellows? Why should I fear them?"

With that he marched up with his arms full of wood, and dropped the wood next to the campfire. One of the men, still with a pistol in his hand, swore and cursed the Mormons again. Then in a loud voice he said to Joseph, "Are you a Mormon?"

Joseph turned to him and answered, "Yes, siree; dyed in the wool; true blue, through and through."

At that, the rough-looking man grabbed him by the hand and said, "Well, you are the %&#$ pleasantest man I ever met! Shake, young fellow, I am glad to see a man that stands up for his convictions."[2]

Words to live by:

Spencer W. Kimball: To hold his testimony, one must bear it often and live worthy of it.[3]

Harold B. Lee: Every member of the church, to be prepared for the millennial reign, must receive a testimony, each for himself, of the divinity of the work established by Joseph Smith.[4]

Joseph F. Smith: Testimony bearing should have a strong educational influence upon the feelings and lives of the children, and it is intended to cultivate within them feelings of thankfulness and appreciation for the blessings they enjoy. The Spirit of God may work within the life of a child and make the child realize and know that this is the work of God. The child knows it is rather because of the Spirit than because of some physical manifestation which he may have witnessed.

Our testimony meetings, then, should have as one of their aims the cultivation of the children's feeling of gratitude not only toward God, but toward their parents, teachers and neighbors. It is advisable, therefore, to cultivate as far as possible their appreciation for the blessings that they enjoy.

Testimony bearing is chiefly for the benefit of those who bear the testimony, in that their gratitude and appreciation are deepened. Testimony bearing is not the accumulation of arguments or evidences solely for the satisfaction and testimony of others.

Let the testimonies, then, of the young people include the training of their feelings by way of making them more appreciative and more thankful for the blessings they enjoy, and the children should be made to understand what these blessings are and how they come to them. It is an excellent way to make people helpful and thankful to others, by first making them thankful to God.[5]

CHAPTER 33

TITHING

*Behold, now it is called today until
the coming of the Son of Man,
and verily it is a day of sacrifice,
and a day for the tithing of my people;
for he that is tithed shall not be burned at his coming.*
D&C 64:23

During the spring of 1899, President Lorenzo Snow was impressed to go to St. George in southern Utah and to take with him as many of the General Authorities as could be spared at Church headquarters. There he would receive a revelation to solve the Church's immediate financial difficulties, providing the solid foundation for the growth that was to occur during the twentieth century.

This vital revelation, however, did not come immediately. Upon arrival in St. George, President Snow paced the floor having "the most painful and anxious expression on his face that I had ever seen," his son, LeRoi C. Snow, later recalled.

"Why have I come to St. George?" President Snow worried aloud. "Why have I come here?"

LeRoi described what happened at the special conference in May 1899, in the St. George Tabernacle. He said, "I was sitting at a table on the stand, reporting the proceedings, when all at once my father paused in his discourse. Complete stillness filled the room. I shall never forget the thrill as long as I live. When he commenced to speak again his voice strengthened and the inspiration of God seemed to come over him, as well as over the entire assembly. His eyes seemed to brighten and his countenance to shine. He was filled with unusual power. Then he revealed to the Latter-day Saints the vision that was before him.

"God manifested to him there and then not only the purpose of the call to visit the Saints in the South, but also President Snow's special mission, the great work for which God had prepared and preserved him, and he unveiled the vision to the people. He told them that he could see, as he had never realized before, how the law of tithing had been neglected by the people.

"The President stressed that faithful compliance with the law would become the means of releasing the Church as well as individual members from the burden of debt. 'The word of the Lord is: The time has now come for every Latter-day Saint, who calculates to be prepared for the future and to hold his feet strong upon a proper foundation, to do the will of the Lord and to pay his tithing in full. That is the word of the Lord to you, and it will be the word of the Lord to every settlement throughout the land of Zion.'

"Referring to the prolonged drought in southern Utah, President Snow assured his listeners that if they would pay an honest tithing they could with faith plant their crops for the coming season. He promised them, in the name of the Lord, 'that the clouds would gather, the rains from heaven descend, their lands would be drenched, and the rivers and ditches filled, and they would reap a bounteous harvest that very season.'"[1]

The Saints followed President Snow's prophetic

counsel and paid their tithing. Soon the rains came again, allowing the crops to flourish, and the Saints in St. George had a large harvest that fall.

President Spencer W. Kimball said, "Tithing is a tenth of income. Inquiries are received at the office of the First Presidency from time to time from officers and members of the Church asking for information as to what is considered a proper tithe. We have uniformly replied that the simplest statement we know of is the statement of the Lord himself, namely, that the members of the Church should pay 'one-tenth of all their interest annually' which is understood to mean income (see D&C 119:4)."[2]

The Lord has promised to bless those who pay their tithing. President Gordon B. Hinckley made a wise statement. He said, "I am not here to say that if you pay an honest tithing you will realize your dream of a fine house, a Rolls Royce, and a condominium in Hawaii. The Lord will open the windows of heaven according to our need, and not according to our greed."[3]

Words to live by:

Spencer W. Kimball: No one is ever too poor to pay tithing, and the Lord has promised that he will open the windows of heaven when we are obedient to his law. He can give us better salaries, he can give us more judgment in the spending of our money. He can give us better health, he can give us greater understanding so that we can get better positions. He can help us so that we can do the things we want to do. However, if we like luxuries or even necessities more than we like obedience, we will miss the blessings which he would like to give us.[4]

Joseph F. Smith: The law of tithing is a test by which the people as individuals shall be proved. Any man who fails to observe this principle shall be known as a man who is indifferent to the welfare of Zion, who neglects his duty as a member of the Church, and who does nothing toward the accomplishment of the temporal advancement of the Kingdom of God. He contributes nothing, either, toward spreading the gospel to the nations of the earth, and he neglects to do that which would entitle him to receive the blessings and ordinances of the gospel.[5]

Lorenzo Snow: A part of a tithing is no tithing at all, no more than immersing only part of a person's body is baptism.[6]

CHAPTER 34

THE WORD OF WISDOM

*Behold, verily, thus saith the Lord unto you:
In consequence of evils and designs which do
and will exist in the hearts of conspiring men
in the last days, I have warned you,
and forewarn you, by giving unto you
this word of wisdom by revelation—*
D&C 89:4

The Lord knew of the challenges that awaited the Saints in the latter days. Doctors are only now proving the dangers that were revealed by the Lord through Joseph Smith nearly two centuries ago. That revelation is now known as Section 89 in the Doctrine and Covenants, and is referred to as the Word of Wisdom.

In 1851 President Brigham Young gave to the Church the Word of Wisdom as a final and definite commandment. From the time it was given to Joseph Smith until 1851, it was considered as a matter of preference or suggestion to the people, a word of advice and counsel. But since 1851 it has been a commandment to all the members of the LDS Church. It is a code of health that blesses a person both physically and spiritually.

President Brigham Young said, "I am as well acquainted with the circumstances which led to the giving of the Word of Wisdom as any man in the Church, although I was not present at the time to witness them.

"The first school of the prophets was held in a small room situated over the Prophet Joseph's kitchen, in a house which belonged to Bishop (Newel K.) Whitney. In the rear of this building was a kitchen, probably ten by fourteen feet, containing rooms and pantries. Over this kitchen was situated the room in which the Prophet received revelations and in which he instructed his brethren.

"The brethren came to that place for hundreds of miles to attend school in a little room probably no larger than eleven by fourteen. When they assembled together in this room after breakfast, the first thing they did was to light their pipes, and while smoking, talk about the great things of the kingdom, and spit all over the room, and as soon as the pipe was out of their mouths a large chew of tobacco would then be taken. Often when the Prophet entered the room to give the school instruction he would find himself in a cloud of tobacco smoke. This, and the complaints of his wife at having to clean so filthy a floor made the Prophet think upon the matter, and he inquired of the Lord relating to the conduct of the elders in using tobacco, and the revelation known as the Word of Wisdom was the result of his inquiry."[1]

The Word of Wisdom deals with various matters. Let's look at them each separately.

Alcoholic drinks

The alcohol advertisements on TV certainly are enticing, as the people on the screen pretend that drinking beer is fun and enjoyable. But it is important to remember one thing: *the people in the ads are actors*. They are being paid to act that way. A more accurate ad would show people the morning after a drinking binge, either too sick to make it to work, or not able to remember what they did.

Make up your mind now to never take that first drink. All around us, in and out of the church, we see people who thought they would experiment a little in the name of fun, but who got addicted and have destroyed their lives.

Another thing you should ponder: Alcoholism is often a hereditary disease. If your ancestors or relatives were susceptible to it, you likely are, too.

President Spencer W. Kimball said, "One of Satan's sharpest tools is alcohol, for it blinds and deafens, numbs and manacles, impoverishes and maims, and kills unfortunate victims. Liquor has been used to neutralize the inhibitions and dull the senses of many a young woman so that her virtue might be more easily taken.

"Alcohol is a crutch for the inadequate. People need help who feel that a party cannot be held, a celebration enjoyed, without liquor. What a sad admission that a party must have liquor for people to have a good time. How barren must some guests be if they must be inebriated!"[2]

Coffee and tea

The Word of Wisdom refers to "hot drinks." President Brigham Young defined that as tea and coffee, and President Kimball has emphasized that again.[3]

Joseph F. Smith told the following story: "Among the least things that we should do is to keep the Word of Wisdom. Brethren and sisters, do not be so weak! I recollect a circumstance that occurred three years ago in a party that I was traveling with. There were one or two who persisted in having their tea and coffee at every place they stopped. I preached the Word of Wisdom right along; but they said, 'What does it matter? Here is Mr. So-and-So, who drinks tea and coffee.'

"Thus the act of one woman or one man nullified not only all that I or my brethren said in relation to it, but also the word of God itself. I said at one time, 'Oh, yes, you say it is a good thing to drink a little tea or coffee, but the Lord says it is not. Which shall I follow?'

"The Lord says that if we will observe the Word of Wisdom we shall have access to great treasures of knowledge, and hidden treasures; we shall run and not be weary, we shall walk and not faint; and the destroying angel shall pass us by, as he did the children of Israel, and not slay us. But the class of men of whom I speak say, in effect, 'We don't care what the Lord says or promises, we will drink tea and coffee anyhow.'

"Such people will set a bad example, no matter what others say or what God has said. They will take the bits in their own mouths, and do as they please, regardless of the effect upon the Saints. I say, out with such practices!"[4]

Drug abuse

Drugs are quickly becoming a major destroyer of families, in and out of the Church. President Gordon B. Hinckley said, "Drugs are a matter of great concern. There has been a great increase in the use of drugs by young people across the United States, a great upsurge. We are feeling it here. We are feeling it everywhere. We need to work on this matter of drugs and helping these boys and girls.

"No boy or girl in this Church should become involved with the use of illegal drugs—not one. They don't need drugs. Drugs will destroy them, they will absolutely destroy them, if they will persist in the use of drugs."[5]

President Hinckley said, "Some have used as an alibi the fact that drugs are not mentioned in the Word of Wisdom. What a miserable excuse. There is likewise no mention of the hazards of diving into an empty swimming pool or of jumping from an overpass onto the freeway."[6]

When speaking of the Word of Wisdom, President Spencer W. Kimball said, "Even sleeping pills, tranquilizers, and such which were thought to be harmless have sometimes brought injury and death; these might well be limited or avoided and, if used at all, taken only under the strict supervision of a reputable physician."[7]

Tobacco

Cigarette smoking has become one of the biggest health threats in modern times. Thousands die each year of lung disease directly caused by smoking. It is addictive—and deadly.

President Kimball said, "A cigarette seems to some such a little thing. But it too is another of the devil's traps. It takes a person away from his best friends, places him in undesirable company. It robs him of the spirit of truth—the gospel and the wholesome influences of proper friends, family, and the Church. It is habit-forming and estranges one from his best interests."[8]

President Joseph F. Smith said, "The use of tobacco in various forms and of strong drinks to some extent is also to be lamented and deplored, especially among the youth, and this evil should be stamped out. The people of God should set their faces like flint against these practices, and they should see to it that their children are taught better, and that a better example is set before them by their parents, in order that the children may grow up without sin in these things."[9]

Words to live by:

Joseph F. Smith: Now, I do wish with all my heart—not because I say it, but because it is written in the word of the Lord—that you would give heed to this Word of Wisdom. It was given unto us "not by commandment"; but by the word of President Brigham Young, it was made a commandment unto the Saints.

It is written here for our guidance, for our happiness and advancement in every principle that pertains to the kingdom of God, in time and throughout eternity, and I pray you to observe it. It will do you good; it will ennoble your souls; it will free your thoughts and your hearts from the spirit of destruction; it will make you feel like God who sustains even the sparrow, that it does not fall to the ground without his notice; it will bring you nearer to the similitude of the Son of God, the Savior of the world, who healed the sick, who made the lame to leap for joy, who restored hearing to the deaf and sight to the blind, who distributed peace, joy, and comfort to all with whom he came in contact, and who cured and destroyed nothing, save it was the barren fig tree, and that was to show forth his power more than anything else:

"And all saints who remember to keep and do these sayings, walking in obedience to the commandments, shall receive health in their navel, and marrow to their bones.

"And shall find wisdom and great treasures of knowledge, even hidden treasures;

"And shall run and not be weary, and shall walk and not faint;

"And I, the Lord, give unto them a promise, that the destroying angel shall pass by them, as the children of Israel, and not slay them."(D&C 89:18-21)

Are these glorious promises not sufficient to induce us to observe this Word of Wisdom? Is there not something here that is worthy our attention? Are not "great treasures" of knowledge, even "hidden treasures," something to be desired? But when I see men and women addicting themselves to the use of tea and coffee, or strong drinks, or tobacco in any form, I say to myself, here are men and women who do not appreciate the promise God has made unto them. They trample it under their feet, and treat it as a thing of naught. They despise the word of God, and go contrary to it in their actions. Then when affliction overtakes them, they are almost ready to curse God, because he will not hear their prayers, and they are left to endure sickness and pain.[10]

BIBLIOGRAPHY

Benson, Ezra Taft. *The Teachings of Ezra Taft Benson.* Salt Lake City, Utah: Bookcraft, 1988.

Benson, Ezra Taft. *To the Young Men of the Priesthood,* pamphlet, Bookcraft, 1986.

Brigham Young University Speeches of the Year. Provo, Utah: Brigham Young University Press, 1960-1966.

Burton, Alma P., *Doctrines From the Prophets,* Cedar Fort, Inc., 1992.

Cannon, George, Q., *Life of Joseph Smith the Prophet,* 1888.

Contributor Magazine, The. Published by The Church of Jesus Christ of Latter-day Saints.

Deseret News. Salt Lake City: Deseret News Publishing Company.

Ensign, The. Published by The Church of Jesus Christ of Latter-day Saints.

General Conference Reports, 1880, 1897-1970.

Grant, Heber J. *Gospel Standards.* Compiled by G. Homer Durham. Salt Lake City: The Improvement Era, 1943.

Hartshorn, Leon R. *Classic Stories From the Lives of Our Prophets,* Salt Lake City, Utah, Deseret Book, 1981.

Hinckley, Gordon B. *The Father, the Son and Holy Ghost,* pamphlet, Bookcraft, 1988.

Hinckley, Gordon B. *The Teachings of Gordon B. Hinckley,* Salt Lake City, Utah, Deseret Book, 1997.

Hunter, Howard W. *The Teachings of Howard W. Hunter.* Edited by Clyde J. Williams. Salt Lake City, Utah: Bookcraft, 1997.

Hymns of The Church of Jesus Christ of Latter-day Saints. Excerpts. Salt Lake City: The Church of Jesus Christ of Latter-day Saints, 1985.

Improvement Era, The. Published by The Church of Jesus Christ of Latter-day Saints.

Instructor, The. Published by The Church of Jesus Christ of Latter-day Saints.

Journal of Discourses. 26 vols. London: Latter-day Saints' Book Depot, 1854-1886.

Juvenile Instructor, The. Published by The Church of Jesus Christ of Latter-day Saints.

Kimball, Edward L., and Andrew E. Kimball, Jr. *Spencer W. Kimball.* Salt Lake City, Utah. Bookcraft, 1977.

Kimball, Spencer W. *The Teachings of Spencer W. Kimball.* Edited by Edward L. Kimball. Salt Lake City, Utah: Bookcraft, 1982.

Kimball, Spencer W. *Faith Precedes the Miracle.* Salt Lake City, Utah: Deseret Book, 1972.

Kimball, Spencer W. *The Miracle of Forgiveness.* Salt Lake City, Utah: Bookcraft, 1969.

Kimball, Spencer W. *Youth of the Noble Birthright.* Salt Lake City, Utah, Deseret Book, 1960.

LDS Church News, Deseret News. Salt Lake City: Deseret News Publishing Company.

Lee, Harold B. *Ye Are the Light of the World: Selected Sermons and Writings of Harold B. Lee.* Salt Lake City: Deseret Book, 1974.

Lee, Harold B. *The Teachings of Harold B. Lee.* Edited by Clyde J. Williams. Salt Lake City, Utah: Bookcraft, 1996.

M Man-Gleaner Manual. Published by the Church of Jesus Christ of Latter-day Saints.

McKay, David O. *Gospel Ideals.* Salt Lake City: The Improvement Era, 1953.

Middlemiss, Clare, comp. *Cherished Experiences from the Writings of President David O. McKay.* Salt Lake City, Utah: Deseret Book Company, 1970.

New Era Magazine, The. Published by the Church of Jesus Christ of Latter-day Saints.

Smith, Eliza R. Snow. *Biography and Family Record of Lorenzo Snow.* Salt Lake City, Utah: Deseret News Company, 1884.

Smith, George Albert, *Sharing the Gospel with Others,* comp. Preston Nibley, Deseret Book, 1948.

Smith, George Albert. *The Teachings of George Albert Smith.* Edited by Robert and Susan McIntosh. Salt Lake City, Utah: Bookcraft, 1996.

Smith, Joseph. *The Teachings of Joseph Smith.* Edited by Larry E. Dahl and Donald Q. Cannon. Salt Lake City, Utah: Bookcraft, 1997.

Smith, Joseph Jr. *History of The Church of Jesus Christ of Latter-day Saints.* Edited by B. H. Roberts. 2d ed., rev. 7 vols. Salt Lake City, Utah: The Church of Jesus Christ of Latter-day Saints, 1932-51.

Smith, Joseph F. *Gospel Doctrine.* Salt Lake City: Deseret Book, 1939.

Smith, Joseph Fielding. *Doctrines of Salvation.* Compiled by Bruce R. McConkie. 3 vols. Salt Lake City, Utah: Bookcraft, 1954-56.

Snow, Lorenzo. *The Teachings of Lorenzo Snow.* Edited by Clyde J. Williams. Salt Lake City, Utah: Bookcraft, 1984.

Talmage, James E. *Jesus the Christ.* 15th ed., rev. Salt Lake City: The Church of Jesus Christ of Latter-day Saints, 1977.

Taylor, John. *The Gospel Kingdom.* Edited by G. Homer Durham. Salt Lake City, Utah: Bookcraft, 1987.

Whitney, Orson F. *Life of Heber C. Kimball: An Apostle—The Father and Founder of the British Mission.* 2nd ed., rev. by Spencer W. Kimball. Salt Lake City: Bookcraft, 1945.

Woodruff, Wilford. *The Discourses of Wilford Woodruff.* Edited by G. Homer Durham. Salt Lake City, Utah: Bookcraft, 1946.

Young, Brigham. *Discourses of Brigham Young.* Compiled by John A. Widtsoe. Salt Lake City: Deseret Book, 1978.

SOURCES

Introduction
1. *Conference Report*, Oct. 1970, 152

Chapter 1—Anger
1. *Ensign*, Nov. 1984, 91
2. *Life of Joseph Smith the Prophet*, 135-137
3. *Ensign*, Nov. 1986, 47
4. *Gospel Doctrine*, 213-214
5. *Journal of Discourses*, 4:98
6. *Journal of Discourses*, 2:93

Chapter 2—Charity
1. *Church News*, Oct. 1, 1988, 16
2. *Juvenile Instructor*, Dec. 1918, 622
3. *Spencer W. Kimball*, 334
4. *Ensign*, Nov. 1985, 85
5. *Teachings of the Prophet Joseph Smith*, 209

Chapter 3—Dancing
1. *Miracle of Forgiveness*, 221-22
2. *Ensign*, Nov. 2000, 52
3. *Juvenile Instructor*, March 1904, 144-145

Chapter 4—Dating
1. *New Era*, Jan. 1975, 38
2. *Ensign*, Feb. 1975, 4
3. *New Era,* Jan. 2001, 13
4. Sydney Australia Area Conference Report, 1976, 54
5. *Ensign,* Nov. 1997, 51
6. *Conference Report*, April 1988, 51-53
7. *Improvement Era*, Sept. 1965, 760
8. *Conference Report*, April 1909, 3
9. *Journal of Discourses*, 8:199-200

Chapter 5—Discouragement
1. *Ensign*, Nov. 1989, 96
2. *Ensign*, Nov. 1988, 6

3. *Improvement Era*, 3:196-197
4. *Conference Report*, April 1899, 2-3
5. *Journal of Discourses*, 9:124

Chapter 6—Education and Employment
1. *Ensign*, Nov. 1975, 122
2. *Classic Stories From the Lives of Our Prophets*, 316
3. Conference in Winnipeg, Manitoba, Canada, Aug. 4, 1998
4. *Ensign*, May 1988, p. 4
5. *Conference Report*, Oct. 1977, 5
6. *Contributor*, 16:570

Chapter 7—Entertainment choices
1. *Conference Report*, Oct. 1972, 106
2. *Ensign*, May 1986, 78
3. *Ensign*, June 1985, 4
4. *Ensign*, Nov. 1975, 39
5. *Conference Report*, Oct. 1903, 98
6. *Ensign*, Nov. 2000, 52
7. Heber City/Springville, Utah, regional conference, 13 May 1995
8. Address to Washington, D.C., chapter of Brigham Young
     Management Society, March 5, 1994
9. *Ensign*, May 1984, 7
10. *Ensign*, May 1978, 45
11. Address to Washington, D.C., chapter of Brigham Young
Management Society, March 5, 1994
12. *Ensign*, May 1979, 4
13. *Improvement Era*, June 1911, 735-8

Chapter 8—Family
1. *Ensign*, May 1988, 52
2. *Conference Report*, Oct. 1974, 161
3. *Sharing the Gospel with Others*, 110-12
4. *Conference Report*, April 1962, 44
5. *Ensign*, Nov. 1980, 4
6. *Ensign*, May 1978, 4
7. *Ensign*, Nov. 1977, 4
8. *Ye Are the Light of the World*, 82
9. BYU Speeches of the Year, April 19, 1961, 5
10. *Conference Report*, April 1964, 5
11. *Improvement Era*, Dec. 1904, 135

Chapter 9—Fasting
1. *Ensign*, Nov. 1985, 85
2. *Ensign*, Nov. 1985, 74
3. *Ensign*, May 1978, 80
4. *Conference Report*, Oct. 1912, 133-34
Chapter 10—Forgiveness
1. *Ensign*, May 2001, 4
2. *Conference Report*, Oct. 1941, 143
3. *Deseret News Church Section*, Jan. 2, 1952, 3
4. *Conference Report*, Oct. 1902, 86
Chapter 11—Friends
1. As told by Gordon B. Hinckley at Santiago Chile Fireside, November 11, 1996
2. Eugene, Oregon, regional conference, Sept. 15, 1996
3. *Instructor*, April 1967, 138
4. *Ensign*, Nov. 2000, 53
5. *The Miracle of Forgiveness*, 221-22
Chapter 12—Gambling
1. *Deseret News*, June 27, 2002, 2
2. *Ensign*, Nov. 1985, 52
3. *Ensign*, May 1975, 5
4. *Improvement Era*, Sept. 1926, 1100
5. *Improvement Era*, Aug. 1908, 807
Chapter 13—Gossip
1. *Ensign*, Nov. 1981, 98
2. *Journal of Discourses*, 19:70
3. *History of the Church*, 3:385
4. *Improvement Era*, March 1903, 388
5. *Juvenile Instructor*, Oct. 15, 1904, 625
6. *History of the Church*, 5:20
Chapter 14—Happiness
1. *Improvement Era*, July 1909, 7440
2. *Ensign*, Nov. 1984, 92
3. *Teachings of Ezra Taft Benson*, 339
4. *Improvement Era*, 1976, 498
5. *Conference Report*, Oct. 1936, 71
6. *Teachings of Lorenzo Snow*, 61

Chapter 15—Heavenly Parents

1. *Journal of Discourses,* 4:54
2. *Biography of Lorenzo Snow,* 46-47
3. *Teachings of the Prophet Joseph Smith,* 34
4. *Hymns of The Church of Jesus Christ of Latter-day Saints, 1985, hymn #292*
5. *Ensign,* November 1991, 100
6. *Journal of Discourses,* 25:51-60

Chapter 16—Holy Ghost

1. *The Father, Son, and Holy Ghost,* 1988
2. *Cherished experiences,* 155-56
3. *Cherished Experiences,* 62-63
4. *Conference Report,* Oct. 1903, 86

Chapter 17—Honesty

1. *Ensign,* Nov. 2000, 53
2. *Improvement Era,* 41:327
3. *Conference Report,* April 1915, 6-7

Chapter 18—Humility

1. *Ensign,* May 1977, 33
2. *Colorado Springs Young Adult Meeting,* April 14, 1996
3. *Improvement Era,* April 1939, 201
4. *Ensign,* May 1979, 34
5. *Conference Report,* 1934, 131
6. *Conference Report,* Oct. 1904, 87-88
7. *Journal of Discourses,* 12: 326-332
8. *Journal of Discourses,* 23:192

Chapter 19—Integrity

1. *Faith Precedes the Miracle,* 241-42
2. *Conference Report,* Oct. 1908, 7
3. *Ensign,* May 2002, 52
4. *Conference Report,* April 1966, 128
5. *Conference Report,* April 1964, 6
6. *Improvement Era,* 1905, 337-339
7. *Journal of Discourses,* 13:218

Chapter 20—Jesus Christ

1. *Jesus the Christ,* 158
2. *Improvement Era,* September 1933, 677
3. *Cherished Experiences,* 101-102

4. *Ensign*, April 1994, 2

5. *Ensign*, Dec. 1988, 2

6. *Ensign*, May 1979, 47

7. Devotional speech given at BYU, May 14, 1957

8. *Juvenile Instructor*, 64:697

9. *Journal of Discourses*, 23:172-173

10. *Journal of Discourses*, 10:217

11. *Journal of Discourses*, 8:339

Chapter 21—Missionary Service

1. *Life of Heber C. Kimball*, 265-266

2. *Ensign*, Oct. 1977, 5

3. *Ensign*, May 1983, 8

4. Youth meeting, Kansas City, Missouri, 14 July 1996

5. *Conference Report*, April 1974, 126

6. *Conference Report*, April 1916, 50-51

7. *Conference Report*, Oct. 1899, 72-73

8. *Conference Report*, April 1898, 31

Chapter 22—Modesty and Fashion Styles

1. Portland Stake Conference, MIA session, Sept. 9, 1956

2. *Improvement Era*, Sept. 1965, 760

3. Portland Stake Conference, MIA session, Sept. 9, 1956

4. *Improvement Era*, Sept. 1965, 760

5. *Ensign*, Nov. 2000, 52

6. *Ensign*, Nov. 2000, 52

7. *Ensign*, May 1988, 92

8. *Improvement Era*, 1976, 449

9. *Journal of Discourses*, 14:18

Chapter 23—Music

1. "60 Years of Radio Broadcasting," Tabernacle Choir
   Broadcast and Program, July 16, 1989

2. Ellen Powell Unthank Monument Dedication, Cedar City,
   Utah, Aug. 5, 1991

3. *Ensign,* Nov. 1986, 84

4. *Conference Report*, Oct. 1899, 68-69

Chapter 24—Patriarchal Blessings

1. *Ensign*, Nov. 1986, 82
2. Smithfield / Logan Utah Regional Conference, April 20, 1996
3. Letter from the First Presidency to Stake Presidents, dated June 28, 1957

Chapter 25—Prayer

1. *Ensign*, Nov. 2000, 53
2. *Ensign*, Nov. 1977, 52
3. *Ensign*, Oct. 1981, 5
4. Meeting, Winnipeg, Manitoba, Canada, Aug. 4, 1998
5. *Conference Report*, Oct. 1923, 7-8
6. *Teachings of Spencer W. Kimball*, 120
7. *Improvement Era*, 47:481
8. *Conference Report*, Oct., 1899, 69-70
9. *Journal of Discourses*, 5:85
10. *Journal of Discourses*, 22:313-15
11. *Journal of Discourses*, 15:36

Chapter 26—Scripture Study

1. *History of the Church*, 4:461
2. *Ensign*, Nov. 1976, 58
3. *To the Young Men of the Priesthood*, 3-4
4. *New Era*, May 1975, 19
5. *Ensign*, Nov. 1977, 4
6. *Conference Report*, Oct. 1961, 18
7. *Conference Report*, Oct. 1917, 41
8. *Conference Report*, Oct. 1913, 9
9. *Journal of Discourses*, 22:335
10. *Discourses of Brigham Young*, 128

Chapter 27—Sexual Purity

1. *Ensign*, Nov. 1996, 49
2. *Ensign*, Nov. 2000, 53
3. Copenhagen Area Conference, Aug. 5, 1976
4. *Ensign*, November 1994, 53
5. *Ensign*, November 1976, 4
6. *Ensign*, Nov. 1980, 94
7. *Youth of the Noble Birthright*, 1960, 91
8. *Conference Report*, April 1971, 82
9. BYU 1987-88 Devotional Speeches, 51

10. Copenhagen Area Conference, Aug. 5, 1976
11. *The Miracle of Forgiveness,* 77
12. *Ensign,* November 1980, 94
13. *Youth of the Noble Birthright,* 1960, 91
14. *The Miracle of Forgiveness,* 65-66
15. *Improvement Era,* June 1918, 738
16. Jordan Utah South regional conference, Mar. 1, 1997
17. Brigham Young University devotional, 17 Oct. 1995
18. Brigham Young University devotional, Sept. 17, 1974
19. *Ensign,* Nov. 1977, 31
20. *Ensign,* Nov. 1980, 94
21. *Juvenile Instructor,* July 1902, 400

Chapter 28—Sabbath Day activities
1. *Improvement Era,* May 1944, 285
2. Meeting with General Authorities and Wives, Oct. 9, 1996
3. Prepared for General Conference, April 6, 1945, but not given
4. *Journal of Discourses,* 14:185
5. *Conference Report,* Oct. 1935, 120
6. *Juvenile Instructor,* 24:87.
7. *Ensign,* Jan. 1982, 3
8. BYU Stake Conference, Jan. 13, 1957
9. Jordan Utah South Regional Conference, March 2, 1997
10. Nottingham England Fireside, Aug. 30, 1985
11. *The Miracle of Forgiveness,* 46
12. *M Man-Gleaner Manual* for 1963-64, 265
13. Smithfield/Logan Utah Regional Conference, April 20, 1996
14. *Ensign,* Jan. 1978, 4
15. *Ensign,* Jan. 1974, 63
16. *Improvement Era,* 1909, 842-844

Chapter 29—Swearing
1. *Improvement Era,* May 1953, 320
2. *Ensign,* Nov. 1987, 47-48
3. *Improvement Era,* May 1903, 501
4. *Doctrines of Salvation,* 1956, 1:13
5. *Improvement Era,* 1967, 420

Chapter 30—Temple Covenants
1. *Journal of Discourses,* 19:229
2. Meeting, Worcester, Massachusetts, 16 Oct. 1998

3. *Improvement Era*, June 1967, 144
4. *Ensign*, May 1988, 51-53
5. Tabernacle Sermon, June 12, 1898
6. M. I. A. Conference, June 5, 1910; Young Woman's Journal, Vol. 21: 456-460
7. *Journal of Discourses*, 22:234
8. Fireside, Lima, Peru, Nov. 9, 1996
9. *Juvenile Instructor*, 39:198
10. *Deseret Weekly*, 50:738
11. *Discourses of Brigham Young*, 416
12. *Teachings of the Prophet Joseph Smith*, 193

Chapter 31—Temptation
1. *Pearl of Great Price*, Joseph Smith History 1:28
2. Varsity Scouts, Arapahoe District, Denver Area Council, July 17, 1993
3. Stockholm Area Conference, youth meeting, Aug. 17, 1974
4. *Improvement Era*, 38:278
5. *Ensign*, April 1984, 9
6. *The Miracle of Forgiveness*, 105
7. *Doctrines From the Prophets*, 416
8. *Conference Report*, Oct. 1948, 82
9. *Juvenile Instructor*, 41:178
10. *Ensign*, Nov. 1984, 35
11. *Ensign*, May 1988, 6
12. *Ensign*, Nov. 1980, 5
13. *Improvement Era*, 1905, 337-339
14. *Journal of Discourses*, 23:192
15. *Journal of Discourses*, 6:98

Chapter 32—Testimony
1. *Conference Report*, Oct. 1960, 108
2. *Gospel Doctrine*, 518
3. *Conference Report*, Oct. 1944, 45
4. *Conference Report*, Oct. 1956, 62
5. *Juvenile Instructor*, April 1903, 246

Chapter 33—Tithing

1. *Improvement Era*, July 1938, 400-1
2. *Ensign*, Nov. 1980, p. 77
3. *Ensign*, May 1982, p. 40
4. Hamburg Stake Conference, Jan. 21, 1962
5. *Conference Report*, April 1900, 47
6. *Teachings of Lorenzo Snow*, 155

Chapter 34—Word of Wisdom

1. *Journal of Discourses*, 12:158
2. *Improvement Era*, Dec. 1967, 52
3. *Ensign*, May 1975, 4
4. *Juvenile Instructor*, December 1902, 721
5. Jordan Utah South regional conference, March 1, 1997
6. *Ensign*, Nov. 1989, 50
7. *The Miracle of Forgiveness*, 57
8. University of Utah Institute, Apr. 14, 1968
9. *Conference Report*, Oct. 1901, 2
10. *Juvenile Instructor*, December 1902, 721

About the Author

Chad Daybell lives in Springville, Utah, with his wife, Tammy, and their five children. He is the author of the *Emma Trilogy*, an exciting LDS fiction series that takes readers into the Wild West, then through the turmoil of World War II, and finally into the future in New Jerusalem.

Chad and Tammy have also written the best-selling *Tiny Talks* series for Primary children.

The Youth of Zion emerged from Chad's years of working with youth as a Scoutmaster and Young Men's advisor. The final inspiration for the book, however, came while Chad was serving as Elders Quorum President and listening to his quorum members struggle to find the right things to say to their teenagers.

One of the quorum members explained that when conflicts formed with his children over certain issues, they would turn as a family to the words of the prophets. A solution was often reached quickly. *The Youth of Zion* is structured for that same purpose—to make the prophets' words more accessible, and to help Church members strengthen their families.

To learn more about Chad and the other books he has written, please visit **www.cdaybell.com**.

9 26575 76313 6